Macarons
& MORE

Publications International, Ltd.

Louis Weber, CEO
Publications International, Ltd.
7373 North Cicero Avenue
Lincolnwood, IL 60712

Photography on pages 5, 7, 11, 13, 15, 17, 21, 25, 27, 29, 31, 33, 35, 37, 39,
41, 43, 45, 47, 49, 51, 53, 55, 57, 59, 61 and 63 by PIL Photo Studio North.
Photography by David Darian and Christopher Hiltz; prop styling by Jenny
Thornton. Recipe testing by Renee Haring, Amanda Kellogg and Jenny Thornton.

Pictured on the front cover: Rosewater Macaron *(page 16),* Double Dark Macaron
(page 12), Saffron Pumpkin Spice Macaron *(page 36),* Chocolate & Vanilla
Macaron *(page 28),* Cosmic Blue Macaron *(page 20),* Honey Pistachio Mascarpone
Macaron *(page 40),* Lime Macaron *(page 6),* Mexican Macaron *(page 34)* and
Peanut Butter & Jam Macaron *(page 54)).*

Pictured on the back cover *(top to bottom):* Chocolate & Vanilla Sandwich
Cookies *(page 86),* Orange Chai Spice Sandwich Cookies *(page 116)* and
Blackberry-White Chocolate Macarons *(page 52).*

ISBN-13: 978-1-4508-5365-1
ISBN-10: 1-4508-5365-X

Library of Congress Control Number: 2012936372

Manufactured in China.

8 7 6 5 4 3 2 1

Microwave Cooking: Microwave ovens vary in wattage. Use the cooking times
as guidelines and check for doneness before adding more time.

Publications International, Ltd.

Table of Contents

Classic Macarons

HAZELNUT MACARONS

MAKES ABOUT 15 MACARONS

Cookies

    1 cup powdered sugar
    ¼ cup almond flour
    3 tablespoons finely ground hazelnuts
    2 egg whites, at room temperature
      Brown paste food coloring
    ¼ cup granulated sugar

Filling

    ½ cup chocolate-hazelnut spread

1. For cookies, line two cookie sheets with parchment paper. Combine powdered sugar, almond flour and halzelnuts in food processor. Pulse into fine powder, scraping bowl occasionally. Sift mixture into medium bowl; discard large pieces.

2. Beat egg whites in large bowl with electric mixer at medium speed until foamy. Beat in food coloring. Gradually add granulated sugar, beating at high speed 2 to 3 minutes or until mixture forms stiff, shiny peaks, scraping bowl occasionally.

3. Add half of flour mixture to egg whites; stir with spatula to combine (about 12 strokes). Repeat with remaining flour mixture. Mix about 15 strokes more by pressing against side of bowl and scooping from bottom until batter is smooth and shiny. Check consistency by dropping spoonful of batter onto plate. It should have a peak which quickly relaxes back into batter. (Do not overmix or undermix.)

4. Attach ½-inch plain tip to piping bag. Scoop batter into bag. Pipe 1-inch circles about 2 inches apart onto prepared cookie sheets. Rap cookie sheets on flat surface to remove air bubbles and set aside. Let macarons rest, uncovered, until tops harden slightly; this takes from 15 minutes on dry days to 1 hour in more humid conditions. Gently touch top of macaron to check. When batter does not stick, macarons are ready to bake.

5. Preheat oven to 350°F. Place rack in center of oven. Bake 13 to 15 minutes, rotating cookie sheets halfway through baking time. Cool completely on cookie sheets. When cooling, if cookies appear to be sticking to parchment, lift parchment edges and spray pan underneath lightly with water. Steam will help release cookies.

6. Match same size cookies; pipe or spread chocolate-hazelnut spread on flat side of one cookie and top with another.

LIME MACARONS

MAKES ABOUT 15 MACARONS

Cookies

- 1 cup powdered sugar
- ¾ cup almond flour
- 2 egg whites, at room temperature
- 2 to 3 drops green liquid food coloring
- ¼ cup granulated sugar
- Grated peel of 2 limes (optional)

Filling

- ¾ cup powdered sugar
- ¼ cup (½ stick) butter, softened
- 1 tablespoon lime juice
- 1 teaspoon vanilla
- ⅛ teaspoon salt
- 1 to 2 drops green liquid food coloring

1. For cookies, line two cookie sheets with parchment paper. Combine 1 cup powdered sugar and almond flour in food processor. Pulse into fine powder, scraping bowl occasionally. Sift mixture into medium bowl; discard large pieces.

2. Beat egg whites in large bowl with electric mixer at medium speed until foamy. Beat in 2 to 3 drops food coloring. Gradually add granulated sugar, beating at high speed 2 to 3 minutes or until mixture forms stiff, shiny peaks, scraping bowl occasionally.

3. Add half of flour mixture to egg whites; stir with spatula to combine (about 12 strokes). Repeat with remaining flour mixture. Mix about 15 strokes more by pressing against side of bowl and scooping from bottom until batter is smooth and shiny. Check consistency by dropping spoonful of batter onto plate. It should have a peak which quickly relaxes back into batter. (Do not overmix or undermix.)

4. Attach ½-inch plain tip to piping bag. Scoop batter into bag. Pipe 1-inch circles about 2 inches apart onto prepared cookie sheets. Rap cookie sheets on flat surface to remove air bubbles. Sprinkle half of macarons with lime peel, if desired. Let macarons rest, uncovered, until tops harden slightly; this takes from 15 minutes on dry days to 1 hour in more humid conditions. Gently touch top of macaron to check. When batter does not stick, macarons are ready to bake.

5. Preheat oven to 350°F. Place rack in center of oven. Bake 13 to 15 minutes, rotating cookie sheets halfway through baking time. Cool completely on cookie sheets. When cooling, if cookies appear to be sticking to parchment, lift parchment edges and spray pan underneath lightly with water. Steam will help release cookies.

6. For filling, beat ¾ cup powdered sugar and butter in large bowl with electric mixer at medium speed 2 minutes or until light and fluffy. Add lime juice, vanilla and salt; beat about 2 minutes or until smooth. Add 1 to 2 drops food coloring; beat until well blended.

7. Match same size cookies; pipe or spread filling on flat side of one cookie and top with another.

Raspberry Macarons
MAKES 16 TO 20 MACARONS

Cookies
- 1½ cups powdered sugar
- 1 cup almond flour
- 3 egg whites, at room temperature
- 1 tablespoon raspberry liqueur
- Red paste food coloring
- ¼ cup granulated sugar

Filling
- Raspberry jam or Chocolate Ganache (page 23)

1. For cookies, line two cookie sheets with parchment paper. Combine powdered sugar and almond flour in food processor. Pulse into fine powder, scraping bowl occasionally. Sift mixture into medium bowl; discard large pieces.

2. Beat egg whites in large bowl with electric mixer at medium speed until foamy. Beat in liqueur and food coloring. Gradually add granulated sugar, beating at high speed 2 to 3 minutes or until mixture forms stiff, shiny peaks, scraping bowl occasionally.

3. Add half of flour mixture to egg whites; stir with spatula to combine (about 12 strokes). Repeat with remaining flour mixture. Mix about 15 strokes more by pressing against side of bowl and scooping from bottom until batter is smooth and shiny. Check consistency by dropping spoonful of batter onto plate. It should have a peak which quickly relaxes back into batter. (Do not overmix or undermix.)

4. Attach ½-inch plain tip to piping bag. Scoop batter into bag. Pipe 1-inch circles about 2 inches apart onto prepared cookie sheets. Rap cookie sheets on flat surface to remove air bubbles and set aside. Let macarons rest, uncovered, until tops harden slightly; this takes from 15 minutes on dry days to 1 hour in more humid conditions. Gently touch top of macaron to check. When batter does not stick, macarons are ready to bake.

5. Preheat oven to 375°F. Place rack in center of oven. Bake 5 minutes, then *reduce heat to 325°F.* Bake 10 to 13 minutes, checking at 5-minute intervals. If cookies begin to brown, cover loosely with foil and reduce oven temperature or prop oven open slightly with wooden spoon. Cool completely on cookie sheets. While cooling, if cookies appear to be sticking to parchment, lift parchment edges and spray pan underneath lightly with water. Steam will help release cookies.

6. Match same size cookies; spread jam on flat side of one cookie and top with another.

ALMOND MACARONS

MAKES ABOUT 15 MACARONS

Cookies

1 cup powdered sugar
½ cup plus 2 tablespoons almond flour
2 egg whites, at room temperature
5 tablespoons granulated sugar

Filling

¾ cup powdered sugar
¼ cup (½ stick) butter, softened
½ teaspoon almond extract

1. For cookies, line two cookie sheets with parchment paper. Combine 1 cup powdered sugar and almond flour in food processor. Pulse into fine powder, scraping bowl occasionally. Sift mixture into medium bowl; discard large pieces.

2. Beat egg whites in large bowl with electric mixer at medium speed until foamy. Gradually add granulated sugar, beating at high speed 2 to 3 minutes or until mixture forms stiff, shiny peaks, scraping bowl occasionally.

3. Add half of flour mixture to egg whites; stir with spatula to combine (about 12 strokes). Repeat with remaining flour mixture. Mix about 15 strokes more by pressing against side of bowl and scooping from bottom until batter is smooth and shiny. Check consistency by dropping spoonful of batter onto plate. It should have a peak which quickly relaxes back into batter. (Do not overmix or undermix.)

4. Attach ½-inch plain tip to piping bag. Scoop batter into bag. Pipe 1-inch circles about 2 inches apart onto prepared cookie sheets. Rap cookie sheets on flat surface to remove air bubbles and set aside. Let macarons rest, uncovered, until tops harden slightly; this takes from 15 minutes on dry days to 1 hour in more humid conditions. Gently touch top of macaron to check. When batter does not stick, macarons are ready to bake.

5. Preheat oven to 350°F. Place rack in center of oven. Bake 15 to 18 minutes, rotating cookie sheets halfway through baking time. Cool completely on cookie sheets. When cooling, if cookies appear to be sticking to parchment, lift parchment edges and spray pan underneath lightly with water. Steam will help release cookies.

6. For filling, beat ¾ cup powdered sugar and butter in large bowl with electric mixer at medium speed 2 minutes or until light and fluffy. Add almond extract; beat until smooth.

7. Match same size cookies; pipe or spread filling on flat side of one cookie and top with another.

Double Dark Macarons

MAKES ABOUT 15 MACARONS

Cookies
- 1 cup powdered sugar
- ½ cup almond flour
- 3 tablespoons unsweetened Dutch process cocoa powder
- 2 egg whites, at room temperature
- 5 tablespoons granulated sugar

Filling
- 2 ounces bittersweet chocolate, finely chopped
- ¼ cup whipping cream
- 1 tablespoon butter

1. For cookies, line two cookie sheets with parchment paper. Combine powdered sugar, almond flour and cocoa in food processor. Pulse into fine powder, scraping bowl occasionally. Sift mixture into medium bowl; discard large pieces.

2. Beat egg whites in large bowl with electric mixer at medium speed until foamy. Gradually add granulated sugar, beating at high speed 2 to 3 minutes or until mixture forms stiff, shiny peaks, scraping bowl occasionally.

3. Add half of flour mixture to egg whites; stir with spatula to combine (about 12 strokes). Repeat with remaining flour mixture. Mix about 15 strokes more by pressing against side of bowl and scooping from bottom until batter is smooth and shiny. Check consistency by dropping spoonful of batter onto plate. It should have a peak which quickly relaxes back into batter. (Do not overmix or undermix.)

4. Attach ½-inch plain tip to piping bag. Scoop batter into bag. Pipe 1-inch circles about 2 inches apart onto prepared cookie sheets. Rap cookie sheets on flat surface to remove air bubbles and set aside. Let macarons rest, uncovered, until tops harden slightly; this takes from 15 minutes on dry days to 1 hour in more humid conditions. Gently touch top of macaron to check. When batter does not stick, macarons are ready to bake.

5. Preheat oven to 350°F. Place rack in center of oven. Bake 13 to 15 minutes, rotating cookie sheets halfway through baking time. Cool completely on cookie sheets. When cooling, if cookies appear to be sticking to parchment, lift parchment edges and spray pan underneath lightly with water. Steam will help release cookies.

6. For filling, place chocolate in medium bowl. Heat cream and butter to a simmer in small saucepan over medium heat; pour over chocolate. Let stand 3 minutes; stir until smooth. Let stand 15 minutes or until spreadable.

12 ❧ Classic Macarons

7. Match same size cookies; pipe or spread filling on flat side of one cookie and top with another.

Lemon Macarons

MAKES ABOUT 15 MACARONS

Filling

- 2 eggs
- 2 egg yolks
- 1 cup granulated sugar
- ⅔ cup lemon juice
- 6 tablespoons butter, softened

Cookies

- 1 cup powdered sugar
- ½ cup plus 2 tablespoons almond flour
- 2 egg whites, at room temperature
- 4 drops purple or yellow gel food coloring
- 5 tablespoons granulated sugar

1. For filling, whisk eggs and egg yolks in small bowl. Combine 1 cup granulated sugar, lemon juice and butter in medium saucepan; cook and stir over medium heat until melted and smooth. Remove from heat. Add egg mixture in thin stream, whisking constantly. Return to low heat; cook and stir 5 minutes or until thickened to pudding consistency. Strain mixture into medium bowl; press plastic wrap on surface. Refrigerate 8 hours or overnight.

2. For cookies, line two cookie sheets with parchment paper. Combine powdered sugar and almond flour in food processor. Pulse into fine powder, scraping bowl occasionally. Sift mixture into medium bowl; discard large pieces.

3. Beat egg whites in large bowl with electric mixer at medium speed until foamy. Beat in food coloring. Gradually add granulated sugar, beating at high speed 2 to 3 minutes or until mixture forms stiff, shiny peaks, scraping bowl occasionally.

4. Add half of flour mixture to egg whites; stir with spatula to combine (about 12 strokes). Repeat with remaining flour mixture. Mix about 15 strokes more by pressing against side of bowl and scooping from bottom until batter is smooth and shiny. Check consistency by dropping spoonful of batter onto plate. It should have a peak which quickly relaxes back into batter. (Do not overmix or undermix.)

5. Attach ½-inch plain tip to piping bag. Scoop batter into bag. Pipe 1-inch circles about 2 inches apart onto prepared cookie sheets. Rap cookie sheets on flat surface to remove air bubbles and set aside. Let macarons rest, uncovered, until tops harden slightly; this takes from 15 minutes on dry days to 1 hour in more humid conditions. Gently touch top of macaron to check. When batter does not stick, macarons are ready to bake.

6. Preheat oven to 350°F. Place rack in center of oven. Bake 15 to 18 minutes, rotating cookie sheets halfway through baking time. Cool completely on cookie sheets. When cooling, if cookies appear to be sticking to parchment, lift parchment edges and spray pan underneath lightly with water. Steam will help release cookies.

7. Match same size cookies; pipe or spread filling on flat side of one cookie and top with another.

Rosewater Macarons

MAKES ABOUT 15 MACARONS

Cookies

1 cup powdered sugar
½ cup plus 2 tablespoons almond flour
2 egg whites, at room temperature
3 drops red liquid food coloring
5 tablespoons granulated sugar

Filling

1 cup powdered sugar
¼ cup (½ stick) butter, softened
1 tablespoon rosewater

1. For cookies, line two cookie sheets with parchment paper. Combine 1 cup powdered sugar and almond flour in food processor. Pulse into fine powder, scraping bowl occasionally. Sift mixture into medium bowl; discard large pieces.

2. Beat egg whites in large bowl with electric mixer at medium speed until foamy. Beat in food coloring. Gradually add granulated sugar, beating at high speed 2 to 3 minutes or until mixture forms stiff, shiny peaks, scraping bowl occasionally.

3. Add half of flour mixture to egg whites; stir with spatula to combine (about 12 strokes). Repeat with remaining flour mixture. Mix about 15 strokes more by pressing against side of bowl and scooping from bottom until batter is smooth and shiny. Check consistency by dropping spoonful of batter onto plate. It should have a peak which quickly relaxes back into batter. (Do not overmix or undermix.)

4. Attach ½-inch plain tip to piping bag. Scoop batter into bag. Pipe 1-inch circles about 2 inches apart onto prepared cookie sheets. Rap cookie sheets on flat surface to remove air bubbles and set aside. Let macarons rest, uncovered, until tops harden slightly; this takes from 15 minutes on dry days to 1 hour in more humid conditions. Gently touch top of macaron to check. When batter does not stick, macarons are ready to bake.

5. Preheat oven to 350°F. Place rack in center of oven. Bake 15 to 18 minutes, rotating cookie sheets halfway through baking time. Cool completely on cookie sheets. When cooling, if cookies appear to be sticking to parchment, lift parchment edges and spray pan underneath lightly with water. Steam will help release cookies.

6. For filling, beat 1 cup powdered sugar and butter in large bowl with electric mixer at medium speed about 2 minutes or until smooth. Beat in rosewater until well blended.

7. Match same size cookies; pipe or spread filling on flat side of one cookie and top with another.

CHOCOLATE MACARONS

MAKES 16 TO 20 MACARONS

Cookies

1 cup powdered sugar
⅔ cup almond flour
3 tablespoons unsweetened cocoa powder
3 egg whites, at room temperature
¼ cup granulated sugar

Filling

Chocolate Ganache (page 23), chocolate-hazelnut spread or raspberry jam

1. For cookies, line two cookie sheets with parchment paper. Combine powdered sugar, almond flour and cocoa in food processor. Pulse into fine powder, scraping bowl occasionally. Sift mixture into medium bowl; discard large pieces.

2. Beat egg whites in large bowl with electric mixer at medium speed until foamy. Gradually add granulated sugar, beating at high speed 2 to 3 minutes or until mixture forms stiff, shiny peaks, scraping bowl occasionally.

3. Add half of flour mixture to egg whites; stir with spatula to combine (about 12 strokes). Repeat with remaining flour mixture. Mix about 15 strokes more by pressing against side of bowl and scooping from bottom until batter is smooth and shiny. Check consistency by dropping spoonful of batter onto plate. It should have a peak which quickly relaxes back into batter. (Do not overmix or undermix.)

4. Attach ½-inch plain tip to piping bag. Scoop batter into bag. Pipe 1-inch circles about 2 inches apart onto prepared cookie sheets. Rap cookie sheets on flat surface to remove air bubbles and set aside. Let macarons rest, uncovered, until tops harden slightly; this takes from 15 minutes on dry days to 1 hour in more humid conditions. Gently touch top of macaron to check. When batter does not stick, macarons are ready to bake.

5. Preheat oven to 375°F. Place rack in center of oven. Bake 5 minutes, then *reduce heat to 325°F.* Bake 10 to 13 minutes, checking at 5-minute intervals. If cookies begin to brown, cover loosely with foil and reduce oven temperature or prop oven open slightly with wooden spoon. Cool completely on cookie sheets. When cooling, if cookies appear to be sticking to parchment, lift parchment edges and spray pan underneath lightly with water. Steam will help release cookies.

6. Match same size cookies; pipe or spread filling on flat side of one cookie and top with another.

Cosmic Blue Macarons
MAKES ABOUT 18 MACARONS

Cookies

    1 cup powdered sugar
    ¾ cup almond flour
    2 egg whites, at room temperature
    ¼ teaspoon teal gel food coloring
    ¼ cup granulated sugar

Filling

    4 ounces cream cheese, softened
    ⅓ cup powdered sugar
    ½ teaspoon vanilla

1. For cookies, line two cookie sheets with parchment paper. Combine 1 cup powdered sugar and almond flour in food processor. Pulse into fine powder, scraping bowl occasionally. Sift mixture into medium bowl; discard large pieces.

2. Beat egg whites in large bowl with electric mixer at medium speed until foamy. Beat in food coloring. Gradually add granulated sugar, beating at high speed 2 to 3 minutes or until mixture forms stiff, shiny peaks, scraping bowl occasionally.

3. Add half of flour mixture to egg whites; stir with spatula to combine (about 12 strokes). Repeat with remaining flour mixture. Mix about 15 strokes more by pressing against side of bowl and scooping from bottom until batter is smooth and shiny. Check consistency by dropping spoonful of batter onto plate. It should have a peak which quickly relaxes back into batter. (Do not overmix or undermix.)

4. Attach ½-inch plain tip to piping bag. Scoop batter into bag. Pipe 1-inch circles about 2 inches apart onto prepared cookie sheets. Rap cookie sheets on flat surface to remove air bubbles and set aside. Let macarons rest, uncovered, until tops harden slightly; this takes from 15 minutes on dry days to 1 hour in more humid conditions. Gently touch top of macaron to check. When batter does not stick, macarons are ready to bake.

5. Preheat oven to 350°F. Place rack in center of oven. Bake 13 to 15 minutes, rotating cookie sheets halfway through baking time. Cool completely on cookie sheets. When cooling, if cookies appear to be sticking to parchment, lift parchment edges and spray pan underneath lightly with water. Steam will help release cookies.

6. For filling, beat cream cheese, ⅓ cup powdered sugar and vanilla in medium bowl with electric mixer at medium speed about 2 minutes or until smooth.

7. Match same size cookies; pipe or spread filling on flat side of one cookie and top with another.

Pistachio Macarons

MAKES 16 TO 20 MACARONS

Cookies

⅓ cup unsalted shelled pistachio nuts
1½ cups powdered sugar
⅔ cup almond flour
3 egg whites, at room temperature
Green paste food coloring
¼ cup granulated sugar

Filling

Chocolate Ganache or Pistachio Filling (page 23)

1. For cookies, line two cookie sheets with parchment paper. Place pistachio nuts in food processor; pulse about 1 minute or until coarsely ground. (Do not overprocess or nuts will form paste.) Add powdered sugar and almond flour to food processor; pulse into fine powder, scraping bowl occasionally. Sift mixture into medium bowl; discard large pieces.

2. Beat egg whites in large bowl with electric mixer at medium speed until foamy. Beat in food coloring. Gradually add granulated sugar, beating 2 to 3 minutes or until mixture forms stiff, shiny peaks, scraping bowl occasionally.

3. Add half of flour mixture to egg whites; stir with spatula to combine (about 12 strokes). Repeat with remaining flour mixture. Mix about 15 strokes more by pressing against side of bowl and scooping from bottom until batter is smooth and shiny. Check consistency by dropping spoonful of batter onto plate. It should have a peak which quickly relaxes back into batter. (Do not overmix or undermix.)

4. Attach ½-inch plain tip to piping bag. Scoop batter into bag. Pipe 1-inch circles about 2 inches apart onto prepared cookie sheets. Rap cookie sheets on flat surface to remove air bubbles and set aside. Let macarons rest, uncovered, until tops harden slightly; this takes from 15 minutes on dry days to 1 hour in more humid conditions. Gently touch top of macaron to check. When batter does not stick, macarons are ready to bake.

5. Preheat oven to 375°F. Place rack in center of oven. Bake 5 minutes, then *reduce heat to 325°F.* Bake 10 to 13 minutes, checking at 5-minute intervals. If cookies begin to brown, cover loosely with foil and reduce oven temperature or prop oven open slightly with wooden spoon. Cool completely on cookie sheets. While cooling, if cookies appear to be sticking to parchment, lift parchment edges and spray pan underneath lightly with water. Steam will help release cookies.

6. Prepare Chocolate Ganache or Pistachio Filling. Match same size cookies; pipe or spread filling on flat side of one cookie and top with another.

Chocolate Ganache: Place 4 ounces chopped semisweet or bittersweet chocolate in medium bowl. Heat ½ cup whipping cream to a simmer in small saucepan over medium heat; pour over chocolate. Let stand 5 minutes; stir until smooth.

Pistachio Filling: Combine 1 cup powdered sugar and ⅓ cup unsalted shelled pistachio nuts in food processor; process 2 to 3 minutes or until coarse paste forms, scraping bowl occasionally. Add 6 tablespoons softened butter and ½ teaspoon vanilla; pulse to combine.

Sophisticated Flavors

SALTED CARAMEL MACARONS
MAKES ABOUT 15 MACARONS

Cookies
- 1 cup powdered sugar
- ½ cup almond flour
- 3 tablespoons unsweetened cocoa powder
- 2 egg whites, at room temperature
- 5 tablespoons granulated sugar

Filling
- 6 tablespoons granulated sugar
- ¼ cup whipping cream
- 2 tablespoons butter
- ½ teaspoon salt
- ¼ teaspoon lemon juice (optional)

1. For cookies, line two cookie sheets with parchment paper. Combine powdered sugar, almond flour and cocoa in food processor. Pulse into fine powder, scraping bowl occasionally. Sift mixture into medium bowl; discard large pieces.

2. Beat egg whites in large bowl with electric mixer at medium speed until foamy. Gradually add 5 tablespoons granulated sugar, beating at high speed 2 to 3 minutes or until mixture forms stiff, shiny peaks, scraping bowl occasionally.

3. Add half of flour mixture to egg whites; stir with spatula to combine (about 12 strokes). Repeat with remaining flour mixture. Mix about 15 strokes more by pressing against side of bowl and scooping from bottom until batter is smooth and shiny. Check consistency by dropping spoonful of batter onto plate. It should have a peak which quickly relaxes back into batter. (Do not overmix or undermix.)

4. Attach ½-inch plain tip to piping bag. Scoop batter into bag. Pipe 1-inch circles about 2 inches apart onto prepared cookie sheets. Rap cookie sheets on flat surface to remove air bubbles and set aside. Let macarons rest, uncovered, until tops harden slightly; this takes from 15 minutes on dry days to 1 hour in more humid conditions. Gently touch top of macaron to check. When batter does not stick, macarons are ready to bake.

5. Preheat oven to 350°F. Place rack in center of oven. Bake 15 to 18 minutes, rotating cookie sheets halfway through baking time. Cool completely on cookie sheets. When cooling, if cookies appear to be sticking to parchment, lift parchment edges and spray pan underneath lightly with water. Steam will help release cookies.

6. For filling, heat 6 tablespoons granulated sugar in large saucepan over medium heat until sugar melts and begins to turn amber, stirring occasionally with wooden spoon. Remove from heat; carefully stir in cream and butter until blended. Stir in salt and lemon juice, if desired. Cool to room temperature.

7. Match same size cookies; pipe or spread filling on flat side of one cookie and top with another.

SESAME & RED BEAN MACARONS

MAKES ABOUT 15 MACARONS

Cookies

- 1 cup powdered sugar
- ½ cup plus 2 tablespoons almond flour
- 2 egg whites, at room temperature
- 5 tablespoons granulated sugar
- 2 teaspoons sesame seeds

Filling

- 4 ounces cream cheese, softened
- ⅓ cup powdered sugar
- ¼ cup red bean paste

1. For cookies, line two cookie sheets with parchment paper. Combine 1 cup powdered sugar and almond flour in food processor. Pulse into fine powder, scraping bowl occasionally. Sift mixture into medium bowl; discard large pieces.

2. Beat egg whites in large bowl with electric mixer at medium speed until foamy. Gradually add granulated sugar, beating at high speed 2 to 3 minutes or until mixture forms stiff, shiny peaks, scraping bowl occasionally.

3. Add half of flour mixture to egg whites; stir with spatula to combine (about 12 strokes). Repeat with remaining flour mixture. Mix about 15 strokes more by pressing against side of bowl and scooping from bottom until batter is smooth and shiny. Check consistency by dropping spoonful of batter onto plate. It should have a peak which quickly relaxes back into batter. (Do not overmix or undermix.)

4. Attach ½-inch plain tip to piping bag. Scoop batter into bag. Pipe 1-inch circles about 2 inches apart onto prepared cookie sheets. Rap cookie sheets on flat surface to remove air bubbles. Sprinkle half of macarons with sesame seeds. Let macarons rest, uncovered, until tops harden slightly; this takes from 15 minutes on dry days to 1 hour in more humid conditions. Gently touch top of macaron to check. When batter does not stick, macarons are ready to bake.

5. Preheat oven to 350°F. Place rack in center of oven. Bake 15 to 18 minutes, rotating cookie sheets halfway through baking time. Cool completely on cookie sheets. When cooling, if cookies appear to be sticking to parchment, lift parchment edges and spray pan underneath lightly with water. Steam will help release cookies.

6. For filling, beat cream cheese, ⅓ cup powdered sugar and red bean paste in large bowl with electric mixer at medium speed about 2 minutes or until smooth.

7. Match same size cookies; pipe or spread filling on flat side of one cookie and top with another.

Chocolate & Vanilla Macarons

MAKES ABOUT 15 MACARONS

Filling

- ½ cup milk
- ⅓ vanilla bean
- ¼ cup granulated sugar
- 1 egg yolk
- 1 tablespoon all-purpose flour
- 2 teaspoons butter

Cookies

- 1 cup powdered sugar
- ½ cup plus 1 tablespoon almond flour
- 3 tablespoons unsweetened cocoa powder
- 2 egg whites, at room temperature
- 5 tablespoons granulated sugar
- 2 tablespoons finely chopped bittersweet chocolate
- 2 tablespoon chocolate toffee bits

1. For filling, combine milk and vanilla bean in medium saucepan; heat over medium heat until bubbles form around edge of pan. Remove from heat; remove and discard vanilla bean. Whisk ¼ cup granulated sugar and egg yolk in medium bowl until light in color. Whisk in all-purpose flour until blended. Slowly add half of milk to egg yolk mixture in thin, steady stream, whisking constantly. Add mixture to remaining milk in saucepan; bring to a boil and boil 1 minute, whisking constantly. Remove from heat; stir in butter. Strain mixture into medium bowl; press plastic wrap on surface. Refrigerate 8 hours or overnight.

2. For cookies, line two cookie sheets with parchment paper. Combine powdered sugar, almond flour and cocoa in food processor. Pulse into fine powder, scraping bowl occasionally. Sift mixture into medium bowl; discard large pieces.

3. Beat egg whites in large bowl with electric mixer at medium speed until foamy. Gradually add 5 tablespoons granulated sugar, beating at high speed 2 to 3 minutes or until mixture forms stiff, shiny peaks, scraping bowl occasionally.

4. Add half of flour mixture to egg whites; stir with spatula to combine (about 12 strokes). Repeat with remaining flour mixture. Mix about 15 strokes more by pressing against side of bowl and scooping from bottom until batter is smooth and shiny. Check consistency by dropping spoonful of batter onto plate. It should have a peak which quickly relaxes back into batter. (Do not overmix or undermix.)

5. Attach ½-inch plain tip to piping bag. Scoop batter into bag. Pipe 1-inch circles about 2 inches apart onto prepared cookie sheets. Rap cookie sheets on flat surface to remove air bubbles. Sprinkle half of macarons with chopped chocolate and toffee bits. Let macarons rest, uncovered, until tops harden slightly; this takes from 15 minutes on dry days to 1 hour in more humid conditions. Gently touch top of macaron to check. When batter does not stick, macarons are ready to bake.

6. Preheat oven to 350°F. Place rack in center of oven. Bake 13 to 15 minutes, rotating cookie sheets halfway through baking time. Cool completely on cookie sheets. When cooling, if cookies appear to be sticking to parchment, lift parchment edges and spray pan underneath lightly with water. Steam will help release cookies.

7. Match same size cookies; pipe or spread filling on flat side of one cookie and top with another.

TIRAMISU MACARONS
MAKES ABOUT 30 MACARONS

Cookies
 1½ cups powdered sugar
 ⅔ cup almond flour
 1 teaspoon espresso powder
 3 egg whites, at room temperature
 1 teaspoon vanilla
 ⅓ cup granulated sugar

Filling
 ¾ cup mascarpone cheese
 6 tablespoons butter, softened
 ½ teaspoon rum extract
 ½ cup powdered sugar
   Unsweetened cocoa powder

1. For cookies, line two cookie sheets with parchment paper. Combine 1½ cups powdered sugar, almond flour and espresso powder in food processor. Pulse into fine powder, scraping bowl occasionally. Sift mixture into medium bowl; discard large pieces.

2. Beat egg whites in large bowl with electric mixer at medium speed until foamy. Beat in vanilla. Granulated add granulated sugar, beating at high speed 2 to 3 minutes or until mixture forms stiff, shiny peaks, scraping bowl occasionally.

3. Add half of flour mixture to egg whites; stir with spatula to combine (about 12 strokes). Repeat with remaining flour mixture. Mix about 15 strokes more by pressing against side of bowl and scooping from bottom until batter is smooth and shiny. Check consistency by dropping spoonful of batter onto plate. It should have a peak which quickly relaxes back into batter. (Do not overmix or undermix.)

4. Attach ½-inch plain tip to piping bag. Scoop batter into bag. Pipe 1-inch circles about 2 inches apart onto prepared cookie sheets. Rap cookie sheets on flat surface to remove air bubbles and set aside. Let macarons rest, uncovered, until tops harden slightly; this takes from 15 minutes on dry days to 1 hour in more humid conditions. Gently touch top of macaron to check. When batter does not stick, macarons are ready to bake.

5. Preheat oven to 350°F. Place rack in center of oven. Bake 13 to 15 minutes, rotating cookie sheets halfway through baking time. Cool completely on cookie sheets. When cooling, if cookies appear to be sticking to parchment, lift parchment edges and spray pan underneath lightly with water. Steam will help release cookies.

6. For filling, beat mascarpone cheese in medium bowl with electric mixer at medium speed about 1 minute or until smooth. Add butter and rum extract; beat 1 minute or until well blended. Gradually add ½ cup powdered sugar, beating about 1 minute or until thick and spreadable.

7. Match same size cookies; pipe or spread filling on flat side of one cookie and top with another. Sprinkle tops of macarons with cocoa.

GREEN TEA MACARONS

MAKES ABOUT 15 MACARONS

Cookies
1 cup powdered sugar
½ cup plus 1 tablespoon almond flour
2¼ teaspoons matcha (green tea) powder
2 egg whites, at room temperature
5 tablespoons granulated sugar

Filling
4 ounces bittersweet or semisweet chocolate chips
¼ cup whipping cream
1 tablespoon butter

1. For cookies, line two cookie sheets with parchment paper. Combine powdered sugar, almond flour and matcha powder in food processor. Pulse into fine powder, scraping bowl occasionally. Sift mixture into medium bowl; discard large pieces.

2. Beat egg whites in large bowl with electric mixer at medium speed until foamy. Gradually add granulated sugar, beating at high speed 2 to 3 minutes or until mixture forms stiff, shiny peaks, scraping bowl occasionally.

3. Add half of flour mixture to egg whites; stir with spatula to combine (about 12 strokes). Repeat with remaining flour mixture. Mix about 15 strokes more by pressing against side of bowl and scooping from bottom until batter is smooth and shiny. Check consistency by dropping spoonful of batter onto plate. It should have a peak which quickly relaxes back into batter. (Do not overmix or undermix.)

4. Attach ½-inch plain tip to piping bag. Scoop batter into bag. Pipe 1-inch circles about 2 inches apart onto prepared cookie sheets. Rap cookie sheets on flat surface to remove air bubbles and set aside. Let macarons rest, uncovered, until tops harden slightly; this takes from 15 minutes on dry days to 1 hour in more humid conditions. Gently touch top of macaron to check. When batter does not stick, macarons are ready to bake.

5. Preheat oven to 350°F. Place rack in center of oven. Bake 15 to 18 minutes, rotating cookie sheets halfway through baking time. Cool completely on cookie sheets. When cooling, if cookies appear to be sticking to parchment, lift parchment edges and spray pan underneath lightly with water. Steam will help release cookies.

6. For filling, place chocolate chips in medium bowl. Heat cream and butter to a simmer in small saucepan; pour over chocolate. Let stand 3 minutes; stir until smooth. Let stand 15 minutes or until spreadable.

7. Match same size cookies; pipe or spread filling on flat side of one cookie and top with another.

Mexican Macarons
MAKES ABOUT 15 MACARONS

Cookies

1 cup powdered sugar
½ cup almond flour
3 tablespoons unsweetened cocoa powder
½ teaspoon ground cinnamon
2 egg whites, at room temperature
¼ cup granulated sugar

Filling

3½ ounces bittersweet chocolate, finely chopped
½ cup whipping cream
2 tablespoons butter
¼ teaspoon ground cinnamon
¼ teaspoon ground red pepper

1. For cookies, line two cookie sheets with parchment paper. Combine powdered sugar, almond flour, cocoa and ½ teaspoon cinnamon in food processor. Pulse into fine powder, scraping bowl occasionally. Sift mixture into medium bowl; discard large pieces.

2. Beat egg whites in large bowl with electric mixer at medium speed until foamy. Gradually add granulated sugar, beating at high speed 2 to 3 minutes or until mixture forms stiff, shiny peaks, scraping bowl occasionally.

3. Add half of flour mixture to egg whites; stir with spatula to combine (about 12 strokes). Repeat with remaining flour mixture. Mix about 15 strokes more by pressing against side of bowl and scooping from bottom until batter is smooth and shiny. Check consistency by dropping spoonful of batter onto plate. It should have a peak which quickly relaxes back into batter. (Do not overmix or undermix.)

4. Attach ½-inch plain tip to piping bag. Scoop batter into bag. Pipe 1-inch circles about 2 inches apart onto prepared cookie sheets. Rap cookie sheets on flat surface to remove air bubbles and set aside. Let macarons rest, uncovered, until tops harden slightly; this takes from 15 minutes on dry days to 1 hour in more humid conditions. Gently touch top of macaron to check. When batter does not stick, macarons are ready to bake.

5. Preheat oven to 350°F. Place rack in center of oven. Bake 13 to 15 minutes, rotating cookie sheets halfway through baking time. Cool completely on cookie sheets. When cooling, if cookies appear to be sticking to parchment, lift parchment edges and spray pan underneath lightly with water. Steam will help release cookies.

6. For filling, place chocolate in medium bowl. Heat cream and butter to a simmer in small saucepan over medium heat. Remove from heat; stir in ¼ teaspoon cinnamon and red pepper. Pour over chocolate. Let stand 3 minutes; stir until smooth. Let stand until thickened.

7. Match same size cookies; pipe or spread filling on flat side of one cookie and top with another.

SAFFRON PUMPKIN SPICE MACARONS

MAKES ABOUT 15 MACARONS

Cookies
   1 cup powdered sugar
   ¾ cup almond flour
   ½ teaspoon saffron threads
   2 egg whites, at room temperature
   ⅛ teaspoon orange gel food coloring
   ¼ cup granulated sugar

Filling
   6 tablespoons cream cheese, softened
   ¼ cup powdered sugar
   2 tablespoons canned solid-pack pumpkin
   ⅛ teaspoon ground cloves

1. For cookies, line two cookie sheets with parchment paper. Combine 1 cup powdered sugar and almond flour in food processor. Pulse into fine powder, scraping bowl occasionally. Sift mixture into medium bowl; discard large pieces. Stir in saffron.

2. Beat egg whites in large bowl with electric mixer at medium speed until foamy. Beat in food coloring. Gradually add granulated sugar, beating at high speed 2 to 3 minutes or until mixture forms stiff, shiny peaks, scraping bowl occasionally.

3. Add half of flour mixture to egg whites. Stir with spatula to combine (about 12 strokes). Repeat with remaining flour mixture. Mix about 15 strokes more by pressing against side of bowl and scooping from bottom until batter is smooth and shiny. Check consistency by dropping spoonful of batter onto plate. It should have a peak which quickly relaxes back into batter. (Do not overmix or undermix.)

4. Attach ½-inch plain tip to piping bag. Scoop batter into bag. Pipe 1-inch circles about 2 inches apart onto prepared cookie sheets. Rap cookie sheets on flat surface to remove air bubbles and set aside. Let macarons rest, uncovered, until tops harden slightly; this takes from 15 minutes on dry days to 1 hour in more humid conditions. Gently touch top of macaron to check. When batter does not stick, macarons are ready to bake.

5. Preheat oven to 350°F. Place rack in center of oven. Bake 13 to 15 minutes, rotating cookie sheets halfway through baking time. Cool completely on cookie sheets. When cooling, if cookies appear to be sticking to parchment, lift parchment edges and spray pan underneath lightly with water. Steam will help release cookies.

6. For filling, beat cream cheese, ¼ cup powdered sugar, pumpkin and cloves in medium bowl with electric mixer at medium speed 2 minutes or until well blended.

7. Match same size cookies; pipe or spread filling on flat side of one cookie and top with another.

TOFFEE MACARONS WITH CHOCOLATE BRANDY FILLING

MAKES ABOUT 15 MACARONS

Cookies
- 1 cup powdered sugar
- ½ cup almond flour
- ¼ cup finely ground pecans
- 2 egg whites, at room temperature
- ⅛ teaspoon brown gel food coloring
- ¼ cup granulated sugar

Filling
- 2½ ounces pitted prunes, cut into quarters (10 to 12 prunes)
- 1½ ounces milk chocolate, chopped
- 1 tablespoon brandy

1. For cookies, line two cookie sheets with parchment paper. Combine powdered sugar, almond flour and ground pecans in food processor. Pulse into fine powder, scraping bowl occasionally. Sift mixture into medium bowl; discard large pieces.

2. Beat egg whites in large bowl with electric mixer at medium speed until foamy. Beat in food coloring. Gradually add granulated sugar, beating at high speed 2 to 3 minutes or until mixture forms stiff, shiny peaks, scraping bowl occasionally.

3. Add half of flour mixture to egg whites; stir with spatula to combine (about 12 strokes). Repeat with remaining flour mixture. Mix about 15 strokes more by pressing against side of bowl and scooping from bottom until batter is smooth and shiny. Check consistency by dropping spoonful of batter onto plate. It should have a peak which quickly relaxes back into batter. (Do not overmix or undermix.)

4. Attach ½-inch plain tip to piping bag. Scoop batter into bag. Pipe 1-inch circles about 2 inches apart onto prepared cookie sheets. Rap cookie sheets on flat surface to remove air bubbles and set aside. Let macarons rest, uncovered, until tops harden slightly; this takes from 15 minutes on dry days to 1 hour in more humid conditions. Gently touch top of macaron to check. When batter does not stick, macarons are ready to bake.

5. Preheat oven to 350°F. Place rack in center of oven. Bake 13 to 15 minutes, rotating cookie sheets halfway through baking time. Cool completely on cookie sheets. When cooling, if cookies appear to be sticking to parchment, lift parchment edges and spray pan underneath lightly with water. Steam will help release cookies.

6. For filling, place prunes in medium bowl. Pour boiling water over prunes to cover; let stand about 5 minutes or until prunes are soft. Drain; squeeze water from prunes. Transfer to food processor; process about 1 minute or until smooth.

7. Place chocolate in small microwavable bowl; microwave on MEDIUM (50%) 1½ minutes, stirring after each 30-second interval, or until chocolate is melted. Stir in brandy. Stir chocolate mixture into prune purée until smooth; cool to room temperature. (Mixture will thicken as it cools.)

8. Match same size cookies; pipe or spread filling on flat side of one cookie and top with another.

Honey Pistachio Mascarpone Macarons

MAKES ABOUT 20 MACARONS

Cookies
- 1 cup powdered sugar
- ⅓ cup almond flour
- ⅓ cup finely ground pistachio nuts
- 2 teaspoons red powdered food coloring
- 2 egg whites, at room temperature
- ¼ cup granulated sugar
- 2 to 3 drops red liquid food coloring
- 2 tablespoons finely chopped pistachio nuts

Filling
- ½ cup mascarpone cheese
- 1 tablespoon honey
- ¼ cup finely ground pistachio nuts

1. For cookies, line two cookie sheets with parchment paper. Combine powdered sugar, almond flour, ⅓ cup ground pistachio nuts and powdered food coloring in food processor. Pulse into fine powder, scraping bowl occasionally. Sift mixture into medium bowl; discard large pieces.

2. Beat egg whites in large bowl with electric mixer at medium speed until foamy. Beat in liquid food coloring. Gradually add granulated sugar, beating at high speed 2 to 3 minutes or until mixture forms stiff, shiny peaks, scraping bowl occasionally.

3. Add half of flour mixture to egg whites; stir with spatula to combine (about 12 strokes). Repeat with remaining flour mixture. Mix about 15 strokes more by pressing against side of bowl and scooping from bottom until batter is smooth and shiny. Check consistency by dropping spoonful of batter onto plate. It should have a peak which quickly relaxes back into batter. (Do not overmix or undermix.)

4. Attach ½-inch plain tip to piping bag. Scoop batter into bag. Pipe 1-inch circles about 2 inches apart onto prepared cookie sheets. Rap cookie sheets on flat surface to remove air bubbles. Sprinkle half of macarons with 2 tablespoons chopped pistachio nuts. Let macarons rest, uncovered, until tops harden slightly; this takes from 15 minutes on dry days to 1 hour in more humid conditions. Gently touch top of macaron to check. When batter does not stick, macarons are ready to bake.

5. Preheat oven to 350°F. Place rack in center of oven. Bake 13 to 15 minutes, rotating cookie sheets halfway through baking time. Cool completely on cookie sheets. When cooling, if cookies appear to be sticking to parchment, lift parchment edges and spray pan underneath lightly with water. Steam will help release cookies.

6. For filling, beat mascarpone cheese and honey in medium bowl with electric mixer at medium speed about 1 minute or until well blended. Fold in ¼ cup ground pistachio nuts. If filling seems too soft to pipe or spread, cover and refrigerate until firm.

7. Match same size cookies; pipe or spread filling on flat side of one cookie and top with another.

Espresso Macarons with Caramel Buttercream

MAKES ABOUT 15 MACARONS

Cookies

- ¾ cup powdered sugar
- ½ cup almond flour
- 2 teaspoons espresso powder
- 2 egg whites, at room temperature
- 1 teaspoon vanilla
- ⅓ cup granulated sugar

Filling

- ¾ cup (1½ sticks) butter, softened, divided
- ¼ cup packed dark brown sugar
- 4 teaspoons light corn syrup
- 2 teaspoons vanilla
- ¼ cup whipping cream
- ¾ cup powdered sugar

1. For cookies, line two cookie sheets with parchment paper. Combine ¾ cup powdered sugar, almond flour and espresso powder in food processor. Pulse into fine powder, scraping bowl occasionally. Sift mixture into medium bowl; discard large pieces.

2. Beat egg whites in large bowl with electric mixer at medium speed until foamy. Beat in 1 teaspoon vanilla. Gradually add granulated sugar, beating at high speed 2 to 3 minutes or until mixture forms stiff, shiny peaks, scraping bowl occasionally.

3. Add half of flour mixture to egg whites; stir with spatula to combine (about 12 strokes). Repeat with remaining flour mixture. Mix about 15 strokes more by pressing against side of bowl and scooping from bottom until batter is smooth and shiny. Check consistency by dropping spoonful of batter onto plate. It should have a peak which quickly relaxes back into batter. (Do not overmix or undermix.)

4. Attach ½-inch plain tip to piping bag. Scoop batter into bag. Pipe 1-inch circles about 2 inches apart onto prepared cookie sheets. Rap cookie sheets on flat surface to remove air bubbles and set aside. Let macarons rest, uncovered, until tops harden slightly; this takes from 15 minutes on dry days to 1 hour in more humid conditions. Gently touch top of macaron to check. When batter does not stick, macarons are ready to bake.

5. Preheat oven to 350°F. Place rack in center of oven. Bake 13 to 15 minutes, rotating cookie sheets halfway through baking time. Cool completely on cookie sheets. When cooling, if cookies appear to be sticking to parchment, lift parchment edges and spray pan underneath lightly with water. Steam will help release cookies.

6. For filling, combine ¼ cup butter, brown sugar, corn syrup and 2 teaspoons vanilla in medium saucepan; bring to a boil over medium heat. Reduce heat to low; simmer 2 to 3 minutes or until thickened. Stir in cream, 1 tablespoon at a time, until caramel reaches consistency of honey. Remove from heat; cool to room temperature.

7. Beat ¾ cup powdered sugar and remaining ½ cup butter in medium bowl with electric mixer at medium speed about 2 minutes or until light and fluffy. Gradually beat in half of caramel until well blended and smooth.

8. Match same size cookies; pipe or spread filling on flat side of one cookie and top with another. Drizzle tops with remaining caramel.

$\mathscr{S}weet$ $\mathscr{S}ensations$

BLUEBERRY MACARONS
MAKES ABOUT 15 MACARONS

Cookies
- 1 cup powdered sugar
- ½ cup plus 2 tablespoons almond flour
- 2 egg whites, at room temperature
- 3 to 4 drops blue gel food coloring
- 5 tablespoons granulated sugar

Filling
- ¾ cup powdered sugar
- ¼ cup (½ stick) butter, softened
- 1½ tablespoons blueberry jam

1. For cookies, line two cookie sheets with parchment paper. Combine 1 cup powdered sugar and almond flour in food processor. Pulse into fine powder, scraping bowl occasionally. Sift mixture into medium bowl; discard large pieces.

2. Beat egg whites in large bowl with electric mixer at medium speed until foamy. Beat in food coloring. Gradually add granulated sugar, beating at high speed 2 to 3 minutes or until mixture forms stiff, shiny peaks, scraping bowl occasionally.

3. Add half of flour mixture to egg whites; stir with spatula to combine (about 12 strokes). Repeat with remaining flour mixture. Mix about 15 strokes more by pressing against side of bowl and scooping from bottom until batter is smooth and shiny. Check consistency by dropping spoonful of batter onto plate. It should have a peak which quickly relaxes back into batter. (Do not overmix or undermix.)

4. Attach ½-inch plain tip to piping bag. Scoop batter into bag. Pipe 1-inch circles about 2 inches apart onto prepared cookie sheets. Rap cookie sheets on flat surface to remove air bubbles and set aside. Let macarons rest, uncovered, until tops harden slightly; this takes from 15 minutes on dry days to 1 hour in more humid conditions. Gently touch top of macaron to check. When batter does not stick, macarons are ready to bake.

5. Preheat oven to 350°F. Place rack in center of oven. Bake 15 to 18 minutes, rotating cookie sheets halfway through baking time. Cool completely on cookie sheets. When cooling, if cookies appear to be sticking to parchment, lift parchment edges and spray pan underneath lightly with water. Steam will help release cookies.

6. For filling, beat ¾ cup powdered sugar and butter in medium bowl with electric mixer at medium speed until smooth. Add jam; beat until blended.

7. Match same size cookies; pipe or spread filling on flat side of one cookie and top with another.

Cookies & Cream Macarons
MAKES ABOUT 15 MACARONS

Cookies
  1 cup powdered sugar
  ½ cup almond flour
  5 chocolate wafer cookies
  2 egg whites, at room temperature
  5 tablespoons granulated sugar

Filling
  ¾ cup powdered sugar
  ¼ cup (½ stick) butter, softened
  3 cream-filled chocolate sandwich cookies, crushed

1. For cookies, line two cookie sheets with parchment paper. Combine 1 cup powdered sugar, almond flour and wafer cookies in food processor. Pulse into fine powder, scraping bowl occasionally. Sift mixture into medium bowl; discard large pieces.

2. Beat egg whites in large bowl with electric mixer at medium speed until foamy. Gradually add granulated sugar, beating at high speed 2 to 3 minutes or until mixture forms stiff, shiny peaks, scraping bowl occasionally.

3. Add half of flour mixture to egg whites; stir with spatula to combine (about 12 strokes). Repeat with remaining flour mixture. Mix about 15 strokes more by pressing against side of bowl and scooping from bottom until batter is smooth and shiny. Check consistency by dropping spoonful of batter onto plate. It should have a peak which quickly relaxes back into batter. (Do not overmix or undermix.)

4. Attach ½-inch plain tip to piping bag. Scoop batter into bag. Pipe 1-inch circles about 2 inches apart onto prepared cookie sheets. Rap cookie sheets on flat surface to remove air bubbles and set aside. Let macarons rest, uncovered, until tops harden slightly; this takes from 15 minutes on dry days to 1 hour in more humid conditions. Gently touch top of macaron to check. When batter does not stick, macarons are ready to bake.

5. Preheat oven to 350°F. Place rack in center of oven. Bake 15 to 18 minutes, rotating cookie sheets halfway through baking time. Cool completely on cookie sheets. When cooling, if cookies appear to be sticking to parchment, lift parchment edges and spray pan underneath lightly with water. Steam will help release cookies.

6. For filling, beat ¾ cup powdered sugar and butter in large bowl with electric mixer at medium speed about 2 minutes or until light and fluffy. Add crushed cookies; beat at low speed until combined.

7. Match same size cookies; pipe or spread filling on flat side of one cookie and top with another.

Black Forest Macarons
MAKES ABOUT 30 MACARONS

Cookies
1½ cups powdered sugar
¾ cup almond flour
3 tablespoons unsweetened cocoa powder
3 egg whites, at room temperature
3 tablespoons granulated sugar

Filling
⅔ cup cherry jam

1. For cookies, line two cookie sheets with parchment paper. Combine powdered sugar, almond flour and cocoa in food processor. Pulse into fine powder, scraping bowl occasionally. Sift mixture into medium bowl; discard large pieces.

2. Beat egg whites in large bowl with electric mixer at medium speed until foamy. Gradually add granulated sugar, beating at high speed 2 to 3 minutes or until mixture forms stiff, shiny peaks, scraping bowl occasionally.

3. Add half of flour mixture to egg whites; stir with spatula to combine (about 12 strokes). Repeat with remaining flour mixture. Mix about 15 strokes more by pressing against side of bowl and scooping from bottom until batter is smooth and shiny. Check consistency by dropping spoonful of batter onto plate. It should have a peak which quickly relaxes back into batter. (Do not overmix or undermix.)

4. Attach ½-inch plain tip to piping bag. Scoop batter into bag. Pipe 1-inch circles about 2 inches apart onto prepared cookie sheets. Rap cookie sheets on flat surface to remove air bubbles and set aside. Let macarons rest, uncovered, until tops harden slightly; this takes from 15 minutes on dry days to 1 hour in more humid conditions. Gently touch top of macaron to check. When batter does not stick, macarons are ready to bake.

5. Preheat oven to 350°F. Place rack in center of oven. Bake 13 to 15 minutes, rotating cookie sheets halfway through baking time. Cool completely on cookie sheets. When cooling, if cookies appear to be sticking to parchment, lift parchment edges and spray pan underneath lightly with water. Steam will help release cookies.

6. Match same size cookies; spread jam on flat side of one cookie and top with another.

Note: These cookies are best eaten within 1 day of baking.

DOUBLE VANILLA MACARONS
MAKES ABOUT 15 MACARONS

Cookies
- 1 cup powdered sugar
- ½ cup plus 1 tablespoon almond flour
- 1 teaspoon yellow powdered food coloring
- 2 egg whites, at room temperature
- ½ vanilla bean, split and seeds scraped
- ¼ cup granulated sugar
- Silver dragées (optional)

Filling
- 2 egg whites, at room temperature
- ¼ cup granulated sugar
- 6 tablespoons butter, softened
- 1 ounce white chocolate, melted and cooled slightly
- ½ teaspoon vanilla

1. For cookies, line two cookie sheets with parchment paper. Combine powdered sugar, almond flour and food coloring in food processor. Pulse into fine powder, scraping bowl occasionally. Sift mixture into medium bowl; discard large pieces.

2. Beat 2 egg whites in medium bowl with electric mixer at medium speed until foamy. Beat in vanilla bean seeds. Gradually add ¼ cup granulated sugar, beating at high speed 2 to 3 minutes or until mixture forms stiff, shiny peaks, scraping bowl occasionally.

3. Add half of flour mixture to egg whites; stir with spatula to combine (about 12 strokes). Repeat with remaining flour mixture. Mix about 15 strokes more by pressing against side of bowl and scooping from bottom until batter is smooth and shiny. Check consistency by dropping spoonful of batter onto plate. It should have a peak which quickly relaxes back into batter. (Do not overmix or undermix.)

4. Attach ½-inch plain tip to piping bag. Scoop batter into bag. Pipe 1-inch circles about 2 inches apart onto prepared cookie sheets. Rap cookie sheets on flat surface to remove air bubbles. Place one silver dragée in center of half of macarons, if desired. Let macarons rest, uncovered, until tops harden slightly; this takes from 15 minutes on dry days to 1 hour in more humid conditions. Gently touch top of macaron to check. When batter does not stick, macarons are ready to bake.

5. Preheat oven to 350°F. Place rack in center of oven. Bake 13 to 15 minutes, rotating cookie sheets halfway through baking time. Cool completely on cookie sheets. When cooling, if cookies appear to be sticking to parchment, lift parchment edges and spray pan underneath lightly with water. Steam will help release cookies.

6. For filling, combine 2 egg whites and ¼ cup granulated sugar in medium bowl set over saucepan of simmering water. Whisk constantly about 3 minutes or until sugar is dissolved and mixture looks like marshmallow cream. Remove from heat; beat with electric mixer at medium speed about 5 minutes or until mixture cools and forms thick, shiny meringue. Add butter, 1 tablespoon at a time, beating until smooth. Beat at medium-high speed 6 to 8 minutes or until thick. Add melted chocolate and vanilla; beat until blended.

7. Match same size cookies; pipe or spread filling on flat side of one cookie and top with another.

BLACKBERRY-WHITE CHOCOLATE MACARONS

MAKES ABOUT 15 MACARONS

Cookies

- 1 cup powdered sugar
- ½ cup plus 2 tablespoons almond flour
- 2 egg whites, at room temperature
- 3 to 4 drops purple gel food coloring
- 5 tablespoons granulated sugar

Filling

- 8 ounces white chocolate chips
- ½ cup whipping cream
- 2 tablespoons butter
- 3 tablespoons blackberry jam

1. For cookies, line two cookie sheets with parchment paper. Combine powdered sugar and almond flour in food processor. Pulse into fine powder, scraping bowl occasionally. Sift mixture into medium bowl; discard large pieces.

2. Beat egg whites in large bowl with electric mixer at medium speed until foamy. Beat in food coloring. Gradually add granulated sugar, beating at high speed 2 to 3 minutes or until mixture forms stiff, shiny peaks, scraping bowl occasionally.

3. Add half of flour mixture to egg whites; stir with spatula to combine (about 12 strokes). Repeat with remaining flour mixture. Mix about 15 strokes more by pressing against side of bowl and scooping from bottom until batter is smooth and shiny. Check consistency by dropping spoonful of batter onto plate. It should have a peak which quickly relaxes back into batter. (Do not overmix or undermix.)

4. Attach ½-inch plain tip to piping bag. Scoop batter into bag. Pipe 1-inch circles about 2 inches apart onto prepared cookie sheets. Rap cookie sheets on flat surface to remove air bubbles and set aside. Let macarons rest, uncovered, until tops harden slightly; this takes from 15 minutes on dry days to 1 hour in more humid conditions. Gently touch top of macaron to check. When batter does not stick, macarons are ready to bake.

5. Preheat oven to 350°F. Place rack in center of oven. Bake 15 to 18 minutes, rotating cookie sheets halfway through baking time. Cool completely on cookie sheets. When cooling, if cookies appear to be sticking to parchment, lift parchment edges and spray pan underneath lightly with water. Steam will help release cookies.

6. For filling, place white chocolate chips in medium bowl. Heat cream and butter to a simmer in small saucepan over medium heat; pour over chocolate. Let stand 3 minutes; stir until smooth. Stir in jam. Let stand 15 minutes or until spreadable.

7. Match same size cookies; pipe or spread filling on flat side of one cookie and top with another.

PEANUT BUTTER & JAM MACARONS

MAKES ABOUT 15 MACARONS

Cookies
- ¼ cup unsalted roasted peanuts
- 1 cup powdered sugar
- ½ cup almond flour
- 2 egg whites, at room temperature
- ½ teaspoon vanilla
- ¼ cup granulated sugar

Filling
- ⅓ cup strawberry or grape jam or orange marmalade

1. For cookies, line two cookie sheets with parchment paper. Place peanuts in food processor; process until finely ground. Add powdered sugar and almond flour; pulse into fine powder, scraping bowl occasionally. Sift mixture into medium bowl; discard large pieces.

2. Beat egg whites in large bowl with electric mixer at medium speed until foamy. Beat in vanilla. Gradually add granulated sugar; beating at high speed 2 to 3 minutes or until mixture forms stiff, shiny peaks, scraping bowl occasionally.

3. Add half of flour mixture to egg whites; stir with spatula to combine (about 12 strokes). Repeat with remaining flour mixture. Mix about 15 strokes more by pressing against side of bowl and scooping from bottom until batter is smooth and shiny. Check consistency by dropping spoonful of batter onto plate. It should have a peak which quickly relaxes back into batter. (Do not overmix or undermix.)

4. Attach ½-inch plain tip to piping bag. Scoop batter into bag. Pipe 1-inch circles about 2 inches apart onto prepared cookie sheets. Rap cookie sheets on flat surface to remove air bubbles and set aside. Let macarons rest, uncovered, until tops harden slightly; this takes from 15 minutes on dry days to 1 hour in more humid conditions. Gently touch top of macaron to check. When batter does not stick, macarons are ready to bake.

5. Preheat oven to 350°F. Place rack in center of oven. Bake 13 to 15 minutes, rotating cookie sheets halfway through baking time. Cool completely on cookie sheets. When cooling, if cookies appear to be sticking to parchment, lift parchment edges and spray pan underneath lightly with water. Steam will help release cookies.

6. Match same size cookies; spread jam on flat side of one cookie and top with another.

Eggnog Macarons

MAKES ABOUT 30 MACARONS

Cookies

- 1 cup plus 2 tablespoons almond flour
- 1 cup powdered sugar
- 2 egg whites, at room temperature
- 2 tablespoons granulated sugar

Filling

- ½ cup granulated sugar
- 2 egg whites, at room temperature
- ¾ cup (1½ sticks) butter, softened
- ¾ teaspoon ground cinnamon
- ¼ teaspoon ground nutmeg, plus additional for garnish

1. For cookies, line two cookie sheets with parchment paper. Combine almond flour and powdered sugar in food processor. Pulse into fine powder, scraping bowl occasionally. Sift mixture into medium bowl; discard large pieces.

2. Beat 2 egg whites in large bowl with electric mixer at medium speed until foamy. Gradually add 2 tablespoons granulated sugar, beating at high speed 2 to 3 minutes or until mixture forms stiff, shiny peaks, scraping bowl occasionally.

3. Add half of flour mixture to egg whites; stir with spatula to combine (about 12 strokes). Repeat with remaining flour mixture. Mix about 15 strokes more by pressing against side of bowl and scooping from bottom until batter is smooth and shiny. Check consistency by dropping spoonful of batter onto plate. It should have a peak which quickly relaxes back into batter. (Do not overmix or undermix.)

4. Attach ½-inch plain tip to piping bag. Scoop batter into bag. Pipe 1-inch circles about 2 inches apart onto prepared cookie sheets. Rap cookie sheets on flat surface to remove air bubbles and set aside. Let macarons rest, uncovered, until tops harden slightly; this takes from 15 minutes on dry days to 1 hour in more humid conditions. Gently touch top of macaron to check. When batter does not stick, macarons are ready to bake.

5. Preheat oven to 350°F. Place rack in center of oven. Bake 13 to 15 minutes, rotating cookie sheets halfway through baking time. Cool completely on cookie sheets. When cooling, if cookies appear to be sticking to parchment, lift parchment edges and spray pan underneath lightly with water. Steam will help release cookies.

6. For filling, combine ½ cup granulated sugar and 2 egg whites in large bowl set over saucepan of simmering water; whisk constantly until sugar dissolves. Remove from heat; beat with whisk attachment of electric mixer at medium speed about 10 minutes or until mixture cools and stiff peaks form. Switch to paddle attachment; add butter, 1 tablespoon at a time, beating until smooth. Beat at medium-high speed until very thick. Beat in cinnamon and ¼ teaspoon nutmeg until blended.

7. Match same size cookies; pipe or spread filling on flat side of one cookie and top with another. Sprinkle tops with additional nutmeg.

LIME MACARONS WITH STRAWBERRY CURD

MAKES ABOUT 15 MACARONS

Cookies
- 1 cup powdered sugar
- ¾ cup almond flour
- 2 egg whites, at room temperature
- Grated peel of 2 limes
- ¼ cup granulated sugar

Filling
- 1 cup sliced strawberries (about 8 medium)
- ¼ cup granulated sugar
- 1 tablespoon cornstarch
- 1 egg yolk, lightly beaten
- 2 teaspoons lemon juice
- 2 tablespoons butter, cut into pieces

1. For cookies, line two cookie sheets with parchment paper. Combine powdered sugar and almond flour in food processor. Pulse into fine powder, scraping bowl occasionally. Sift mixture into medium bowl; discard large pieces.

2. Beat egg whites in large bowl with electric mixer at medium speed until foamy. Beat in lime peel. Gradually add ¼ cup granulated sugar, beating at high speed 2 to 3 minutes or until mixture forms stiff, shiny peaks, scraping bowl occasionally.

3. Add half of flour mixture to egg whites; stir with spatula to combine (about 12 strokes). Repeat with remaining flour mixture. Mix about 15 strokes more by pressing against side of bowl and scooping from bottom until batter is smooth and shiny. Check consistency by dropping spoonful of batter onto plate. It should have a peak which quickly relaxes back into batter. (Do not overmix or undermix.)

4. Attach ½-inch plain tip to piping bag. Scoop batter into bag. Pipe 1-inch circles about 2 inches apart onto prepared cookie sheets. Rap cookie sheets on flat surface to remove air bubbles and set aside. Let macarons rest, uncovered, until tops harden slightly; this takes from 15 minutes on dry days to 1 hour in more humid conditions. Gently touch top of macaron to check. When batter does not stick, macarons are ready to bake.

5. Preheat oven to 350°F. Place rack in center of oven. Bake 13 to 15 minutes, rotating cookie sheets halfway through baking time. Cool completely on cookie sheets. When cooling, if cookies appear to be sticking to parchment, lift parchment edges and spray pan underneath lightly with water. Steam will help release cookies.

6. For filling, place strawberries in food processor or blender; process about 30 seconds or until smooth. Strain purée to remove seeds. Combine strawberry purée, ¼ cup granulated sugar, cornstarch, egg yolk and lemon juice in medium heavy saucepan; cook over medium heat 6 to 7 minutes or until very thick, whisking constantly. Remove from heat; gradually whisk in butter until melted. Let cool to room temperature.

7. Match same size cookies; pipe or spread filling on flat side of one cookie and top with another.

CHOCOLATE PEPPERMINT MACARONS
MAKES ABOUT 15 MACARONS

Cookies
- 1 cup powdered sugar
- ½ cup almond flour
- 3 tablespoons unsweetened cocoa powder
- 2 egg whites, at room temperature
- Brown gel food coloring (optional)
- 5 tablespoons granulated sugar

Filling
- ¾ cup powdered sugar
- ¼ cup (½ stick) butter, softened
- ¼ to ½ teaspoon peppermint extract
- Green liquid food coloring

1. For cookies, line two cookie sheets with parchment paper. Combine 1 cup powdered sugar, almond flour and cocoa in food processor. Pulse into fine powder, scraping bowl occasionally. Sift mixture into medium bowl; discard large pieces.

2. Beat egg whites in large bowl with electric mixer at medium speed until foamy. Beat in brown food coloring, if desired. Gradually add granulated sugar, beating at high speed 2 to 3 minutes or until mixture forms stiff, shiny peaks, scraping bowl occasionally.

3. Add half of flour mixture to egg whites; stir with spatula to combine (about 12 strokes). Repeat with remaining flour mixture. Mix about 15 strokes more by pressing against side of bowl and scooping from bottom until batter is smooth and shiny. Check consistency by dropping spoonful of batter onto plate. It should have a peak which quickly relaxes back into batter. (Do not overmix or undermix.)

4. Attach ½-inch plain tip to piping bag. Scoop batter into bag. Pipe 1-inch circles about 2 inches apart onto prepared cookie sheets. Rap cookie sheets on flat surface to remove air bubbles and set aside. Let macarons rest, uncovered, until tops harden slightly; this takes from 15 minutes on dry days to 1 hour in more humid conditions. Gently touch top of macaron to check. When batter does not stick, macarons are ready to bake.

5. Preheat oven to 350°F. Place rack in center of oven. Bake 15 to 18 minutes, rotating cookie sheets halfway through baking time. Cool completely on cookie sheets. When cooling, if cookies appear to be sticking to parchment, lift parchment edges and spray pan underneath lightly with water. Steam will help release cookies.

6. For filling, beat ¾ cup powdered sugar and butter in large bowl with electric mixer at medium speed about 2 minutes or until light and fluffy. Add peppermint extract and green food coloring; beat until smooth.

7. Match same size cookies; pipe or spread filling on flat side of one cookie and top with another.

Vanilla Orange Macarons

MAKES ABOUT 15 MACARONS

Cookies

- 1 cup plus 1 tablespoon powdered sugar
- ¾ cup almond flour
- 1 teaspoon orange powdered food coloring
- 2 egg whites, at room temperature
- ¼ teaspoon vanilla
- ¼ cup granulated sugar

Filling

- ⅓ cup orange marmalade

1. For cookies, line two cookie sheets with parchment paper. Combine powdered sugar, almond flour and food coloring in food processor. Pulse into fine powder, scraping bowl occasionally. Sift mixture into medium bowl; discard large pieces.

2. Beat egg whites in large bowl with electric mixer at medium speed until foamy. Beat in vanilla. Gradually add granulated sugar, beating at high speed 2 to 3 minutes or until mixture forms stiff, shiny peaks, scraping bowl occasionally.

3. Add half of flour mixture to egg whites. Stir with spatula to combine (about 12 strokes). Repeat with remaining flour mixture. Mix about 15 strokes more by pressing against side of bowl and scooping from bottom until batter is smooth and shiny. Check consistency by dropping spoonful of batter onto plate. It should have a peak which quickly relaxes back into batter. (Do not overmix or undermix.)

4. Attach ½-inch plain tip to piping bag. Scoop batter into bag. Pipe 1-inch circles about 2 inches apart onto prepared cookie sheets. Rap cookie sheets on flat surface to remove air bubbles and set aside. Let macarons rest, uncovered, until tops harden slightly; this takes from 15 minutes on dry days to 1 hour in more humid conditions. Gently touch top of macaron to check. When batter does not stick, macarons are ready to bake.

5. Preheat oven to 350°F. Place rack in center of oven. Bake 13 to 15 minutes, rotating cookie sheets halfway through baking time. Cool completely on cookie sheets. When cooling, if cookies appear to be sticking to parchment, lift parchment edges and spray pan underneath lightly with water. Steam will help release cookies.

6. Match same size cookies; spread marmalade on flat side of one cookie and top with another.

Super Sandwiches

Banana Sandies

MAKES ABOUT 24 SANDWICH COOKIES

2⅓ cups all-purpose flour
1 cup (2 sticks) butter, softened
¾ cup granulated sugar
¼ cup packed brown sugar
1 medium banana, cut into ¼-inch slices
1 teaspoon vanilla
¼ teaspoon salt
⅔ cup chopped pecans
Prepared cream cheese frosting
Yellow food coloring (optional)

1. Preheat oven to 350°F. Grease cookie sheets or line with parchment paper.

2. Beat flour, butter, granulated sugar, brown sugar, banana, vanilla and salt in large bowl with electric mixer 2 to 3 minutes or until well blended. Stir in pecans.

3. Shape dough into 1-inch balls; place 2 inches apart on prepared cookie sheets. Flatten to ¼-inch thickness with bottom of glass dipped in sugar.

4. Bake 12 to 15 minutes or until edges are lightly browned. Remove to wire racks; cool completely.

5. Tint frosting with food coloring, if desired. Pipe or spread 1 tablespoon frosting on flat side of half of cookies; top with remaining cookies.

TINY PEANUT BUTTER SANDWICHES

MAKES 6 TO 7 DOZEN SANDWICH COOKIES

1¼ cups all-purpose flour
½ teaspoon baking powder
½ teaspoon baking soda
¼ teaspoon salt
½ cup granulated sugar
½ cup packed brown sugar
½ cup (1 stick) butter, softened
½ cup creamy peanut butter
1 egg
1 teaspoon vanilla
1 cup semisweet chocolate chips
½ cup whipping cream

1. For cookies, preheat oven to 350°F. Combine flour, baking powder, baking soda and salt in medium bowl.

2. Beat granulated sugar, brown sugar and butter in large bowl with electric mixer at medium speed until light and fluffy. Beat in peanut butter, egg and vanilla until well blended. Gradually beat in flour mixture at low speed until blended.

3. Shape dough by ½ teaspoonfuls into balls; place 1 inch apart on ungreased cookie sheets. Flatten balls slightly with fork in criss-cross pattern.

4. Bake 6 minutes or just until set. Cool on cookie sheets 4 minutes. Remove to wire racks; cool completely.

5. For filling, place chocolate chips in medium bowl. Place cream in small microwavable bowl; microwave on HIGH 2 minutes or just until simmering. Pour over chocolate chips. Let stand 3 minutes; stir until smooth. Let stand 10 minutes or until filling thickens to desired consistency.

6. Pipe or spread scant teaspoon filling on flat side of half of cookies; top with remaining cookies. Store in airtight container.

SUNSHINE SANDWICHES

MAKES ABOUT 24 SANDWICH COOKIES

⅓ cup coarse or granulated sugar
¾ cup (1½ sticks) plus 2 tablespoons butter, softened, divided
1 egg
2 tablespoons grated lemon peel
1 package (about 18 ounces) lemon cake mix with pudding
    in the mix
¼ cup yellow cornmeal
2 cups sifted powdered sugar
2 to 3 tablespoons lemon juice

1. For cookies, preheat oven to 375°F. Place coarse sugar in shallow bowl.

2. Beat ¾ cup butter in large bowl with electric mixer at medium speed until light and fluffy. Add egg and lemon peel; beat 30 seconds. Add cake mix, one third at a time, beating at low speed after each addition until blended. Stir in cornmeal. (Dough will be stiff.)

3. Shape dough into 1-inch balls; roll in coarse sugar. Place 2 inches apart on ungreased cookie sheets.

4. Bake 8 to 9 minutes or until edges are lightly browned. Cool on cookie sheets 1 minute. Remove to wire racks; cool completely.

5. For filling, beat powdered sugar and remaining 2 tablespoons butter in large bowl with electric mixer at medium speed until blended. Gradually add enough lemon juice to reach spreading consistency.

6. Pipe or spread about 1 teaspoon filling on flat side of half of cookies; top with remaining cookies. Store covered at room temperature up to 24 hours or freeze up to 3 months.

CINNAMON RAISIN DELIGHTS

MAKES ABOUT 12 SANDWICH COOKIES

1¼ cups all-purpose flour
1 teaspoon ground cinnamon
½ teaspoon salt
½ teaspoon baking soda
½ cup (1 stick) butter, softened
½ cup packed brown sugar
¼ cup granulated sugar
1 egg, lightly beaten
1 teaspoon vanilla
1 cup raisins
¾ cup prepared vanilla frosting

1. Preheat oven to 350°F. Lightly grease cookie sheets. Combine flour, cinnamon, salt and baking soda in medium bowl.

2. Beat butter, brown sugar and granulated sugar in large bowl with electric mixer at medium speed until light and fluffy. Add egg and vanilla; beat until well blended. Add flour mixture; beat just until blended. Stir in raisins.

3. Shape dough by rounded tablespoonfuls into balls; place 2 inches apart on prepared cookie sheets.

4. Bake 11 to 13 minutes or until edges are lightly browned. Cool on cookie sheets 2 minutes. Remove to wire racks; cool completely.

5. Pipe or spread 1 tablespoon frosting on flat side of half of cookies; top with remaining cookies.

Peanut Butter S'Mores

MAKES 16 SANDWICH COOKIES

1½ cups all-purpose flour
½ teaspoon baking powder
½ teaspoon baking soda
¼ teaspoon salt
½ cup (1 stick) butter, softened
½ cup granulated sugar
½ cup packed brown sugar
½ cup creamy or chunky peanut butter
1 egg
1 teaspoon vanilla
½ cup chopped roasted peanuts (optional)
4 (1.55-ounce) milk chocolate candy bars
16 large marshmallows

1. Preheat oven to 350°F. Combine flour, baking powder, baking soda and salt in small bowl.

2. Beat butter, granulated sugar and brown sugar in large bowl with electric mixer at medium speed until light and fluffy. Beat in peanut butter, egg and vanilla until well blended. Gradually beat in flour mixture at low speed until blended. Stir in peanuts, if desired.

3. Shape dough into 1-inch balls; place 2 inches apart on ungreased cookie sheets. Flatten balls slightly with fork in criss-cross pattern.

4. Bake 14 minutes or until set and edges are lightly browned. Cool on cookie sheets 2 minutes. Remove to wire racks; cool completely.

5. Break each candy bar into four sections. Place 1 section of chocolate on flat side of 1 cookie. Place on microwavable plate; top with 1 marshmallow. Microwave on HIGH 10 to 12 seconds or until marshmallow is puffy. Immediately top with another cookie, flat side down, pressing lightly to spread marshmallow to edges. Repeat with remaining cookies, chocolate and marshmallows, one at a time. Cool completely.

Orange Dreams

MAKES ABOUT 24 SANDWICH COOKIES

2½ cups all-purpose flour
¼ teaspoon baking powder
¼ teaspoon baking soda
¼ teaspoon salt
2½ cups powdered sugar, divided
1 cup (2 sticks) butter, softened
1 egg
4 tablespoons orange juice, divided
1½ tablespoons plus 1 teaspoon finely grated orange peel, divided
2 teaspoons vanilla
1 teaspoon lemon juice
1 teaspoon orange extract
Red and yellow food coloring (optional)
1 container (16 ounces) vanilla frosting
Candied orange peel strips (optional)

1. For cookies, combine flour, baking powder, baking soda and salt in small bowl. Beat 1 cup powdered sugar and butter in large bowl with electric mixer at medium speed 2 minutes or until creamy. Add egg, 2 tablespoons orange juice, 1½ tablespoons orange peel, vanilla, lemon juice and orange extract; beat until well blended. Gradually beat in flour mixture just until blended.

2. Shape dough into two logs about 2 inches in diameter on lightly floured surface. Wrap tightly in waxed paper; refrigerate 3 hours or overnight.

3. Preheat oven to 350°F. Grease cookie sheets. Cut each log into ¼-inch-thick slices; place 1 inch apart on prepared cookie sheets.

4. Bake 10 minutes or until edges are lightly browned. Cool on cookie sheets 2 minutes. Remove to wire racks; cool completely.

5. For glaze, whisk remaining 1½ cups powdered sugar, 2 tablespoons orange juice and 1 teaspoon orange peel in medium bowl until blended. Add additional orange juice, if necessary, to reached desired glaze consistency. Add several drops food coloring to tint glaze, if desired.

6. Spread glaze over tops of half of cookies; top with candied orange peel, if desired. Let stand 1 hour or until glaze is set. Pipe or spread frosting on flat side of unglazed cookies; top with glazed cookies. Store loosely covered in single layer up to 1 week or freeze up to 1 month.

Pumpkin Chocolate Chip Sandwiches

MAKES ABOUT 24 SANDWICH COOKIES

1 cup canned solid-pack pumpkin
1 package (about 16 ounces) refrigerated chocolate chip
    cookie dough
¾ cup all-purpose flour
½ teaspoon pumpkin pie spice*
½ cup prepared cream cheese frosting

*Or substitute ¼ teaspoon ground cinnamon, ⅛ teaspoon ground ginger and pinch
each of ground allspice and ground nutmeg.

1. Line colander with paper towel. Place pumpkin in colander; drain
about 20 minutes to remove excess moisture.

2. Let dough stand at room temperature 15 minutes. Preheat oven
to 350°F. Grease cookie sheets.

3. Beat dough, pumpkin, flour and pumpkin pie spice in large bowl
with electric mixer at medium speed until well blended. Drop dough
by rounded teaspoonfuls 2 inches apart onto prepared cookie sheets.

4. Bake 9 to 11 minutes or until set. Cool on cookie sheets 3 minutes.
Remove to wire racks; cool completely.

5. Pipe or spread about 1 teaspoon frosting on flat side of half of cookies;
top with remaining cookies.

Chocolate Almond Sandwiches

MAKES ABOUT 30 SANDWICH COOKIES

1 package (about 16 ounces) refrigerated sugar cookie dough
4 ounces almond paste
¼ cup all-purpose flour
1 container (16 ounces) dark chocolate frosting
   Sliced almonds

1. Let dough stand at room temperature 15 minutes.

2. Beat dough, almond paste and flour in large bowl with electric mixer at medium speed until well blended. Divide dough into three pieces; wrap in plastic wrap and freeze 20 minutes. Shape each piece into 10-inch log. Wrap tightly in plastic wrap; refrigerate at least 2 hours or overnight. (Or freeze 1 hour or until firm.)

3. Preheat oven to 350°F. Lightly grease cookie sheets. Cut each log into ⅜-inch-thick slices; place 2 inches apart on prepared cookie sheets.

4. Bake 10 to 12 minutes or until edges are lightly browned. Cool on cookie sheets 2 minutes. Remove to wire racks; cool completely.

5. Pipe or spread 2 teaspoons frosting on flat side of half of cookies; top with remaining cookies. Spread small amount of frosting on top of each sandwich cookie; top with sliced almond.

Note: Almond paste is a prepared product made of ground blanched almonds, sugar and an ingredient such as glucose, glycerin or corn syrup to keep it pliable. It is often used as an ingredient in confections and baked goods. Almond paste is available in cans and plastic tubes in most supermarkets or gourmet food markets. After opening, wrap the container tightly and store it in the refrigerator.

PB & J Sandwich Cookies

MAKES ABOUT 30 SANDWICH COOKIES

1 cup (2 sticks) plus 2 tablespoons butter, softened, divided
1½ cups powdered sugar, divided
2 tablespoons packed brown sugar
¼ teaspoon salt
2 cups all-purpose flour
⅓ cup plus 2 tablespoons creamy peanut butter, divided
2 tablespoons strawberry jam
3 to 4 drops red food coloring
3 tablespoons milk or half-and-half

1. For cookies, beat 1 cup butter, ½ cup powdered sugar, brown sugar and salt in large bowl with electric mixer at medium speed 2 minutes or until light and fluffy. Gradually add flour, beating well after each addition.

2. Divide dough in half. Add 2 tablespoons peanut butter to half of dough; beat until blended. Shape peanut butter dough into 10-inch log. Wrap in plastic wrap; refrigerate 1 hour. Add jam and food coloring to remaining half of dough; beat until blended. Shape strawberry dough into 10-inch log. Wrap in plastic wrap; refrigerate 1 hour.

3. Preheat oven to 300°F. Cut each log into ⅓-inch-thick slices; place on ungreased cookie sheets.

4. Bake 15 to 18 minutes or until set and lightly browned. Cool on cookie sheets 5 minutes. Remove to wire racks; cool completely.

5. For filling, beat remaining ⅓ cup peanut butter and 2 tablespoons butter in large bowl with electric mixer at medium speed until smooth. Gradually add remaining 1 cup powdered sugar; beat until blended. Add milk; beat until light and fluffy.

6. Spread about 1½ teaspoons filling on flat side of peanut butter cookies; top with strawberry cookies.

MINT CANDY SANDWICHES

MAKES ABOUT 30 SANDWICH COOKIES

1 package (4.67 ounces) chocolate crème de menthe candy wafers, divided
1¼ cups all-purpose flour
½ teaspoon salt
½ teaspoon baking soda
½ cup (1 stick) butter, softened
½ cup granulated sugar
¼ cup packed brown sugar
1 egg, lightly beaten
1 teaspoon vanilla
4 ounces cream cheese, softened
Melted semisweet and/or white chocolate (optional)

1. For cookies, preheat oven to 350°F. Lightly grease cookie sheets. Chop 8 candy wafers to measure about ⅓ cup. Combine flour, salt and baking soda in medium bowl.

2. Beat butter, granulated sugar and brown sugar in large bowl with electric mixer until light and fluffy. Add egg and vanilla; beat until well blended. Add flour mixture; beat just until blended. Stir in chopped candy wafers.

3. Shape dough by rounded teaspoonfuls into balls; place 2 inches apart on prepared cookie sheets.

4. Bake 8 minutes or until edges are lightly browned. Cool on cookie sheets 1 minute. Remove to wire racks; cool completely.

5. For filling, place remaining candy wafers in medium microwavable bowl. Microwave on HIGH 30 seconds; stir. Microwave at additional 30-second intervals until candy is melted and smooth when stirred. Beat cream cheese in large bowl with electric mixer until light and fluffy. Add melted candy; beat until well blended.

6. Spread small amount of filling on flat side of half of cookies; top with remaining cookies. Drizzle sandwiches with chocolate, if desired. Let stand until chocolate is set.

Peanut Butter Ice Cream Triangles

MAKES ABOUT 10 ICE CREAM SANDWICHES

1½ cups all-purpose flour
½ teaspoon baking powder
½ teaspoon baking soda
¼ teaspoon salt
½ cup granulated sugar
½ cup packed brown sugar
½ cup (1 stick) butter, softened
½ cup creamy peanut butter
1 egg
1 teaspoon vanilla
2½ to 3 cups vanilla, cinnamon or chocolate ice cream, softened

1. Preheat oven to 350°F. Grease cookie sheets. Combine flour, baking powder, baking soda and salt in medium bowl.

2. Beat granulated sugar, brown sugar and butter in large bowl with electric mixer at medium speed until light and fluffy. Beat in peanut butter, egg and vanilla until well blended. Gradually beat in flour mixture at low speed until blended.

3. Divide dough in half. Roll each half of dough between 2 sheets of waxed paper or plastic wrap into 10-inch square, about ⅛ inch thick. Remove top sheet of waxed paper; invert dough onto prepared cookie sheet. Remove second sheet of waxed paper.

4. Score dough into four squares. Score each square diagonally into two triangles. *Do not cut completely through dough.* Combine excess scraps of dough; roll out and score into additional triangles.

5. Bake 12 to 13 minutes or until set and edges are golden brown. Cool on cookie sheets 2 minutes. Cut through score marks with knife; cool completely on cookie sheets.

6. Place half of cookies on flat surface. Spread ¼ to ⅓ cup softened ice cream on flat side of half of cookies; top with remaining cookies. Wrap in plastic wrap; freeze 1 hour or up to 2 days.

BLACK & WHITE SANDWICH COOKIES

MAKES 36 SANDWICH COOKIES

1 package (about 18 ounces) chocolate cake mix with pudding in the mix
1½ cups (3 sticks) butter, softened, divided
2 egg yolks, divided
½ to ¾ cup milk, divided
1 package (about 18 ounces) butter recipe yellow cake mix with pudding in the mix
4 cups powdered sugar
¼ teaspoon salt

1. Preheat oven to 325°F.

2. For chocolate cookies, place half of chocolate cake mix in large bowl. Add ½ cup butter; beat with electric mixer at medium speed until well blended. Add 1 egg yolk and remaining chocolate cake mix; beat just until dough forms. Beat in 1 to 2 tablespoons milk if dough is too crumbly.

3. Shape dough by rounded tablespoonfuls into 36 balls; place 2 inches apart on ungreased cookie sheets and flatten slightly. Bake 20 minutes or until set. Cool on cookie sheets 5 minutes. Remove to wire racks; cool completely.

4. For vanilla cookies, place half of yellow cake mix in large bowl. Add ½ cup butter; beat with electric mixer at medium speed until well blended. Add remaining egg yolk and yellow cake mix; beat just until dough forms. Beat in 1 to 2 tablespoons milk if dough is too crumbly.

5. Shape dough by rounded tablespoonfuls into 36 balls; place 2 inches apart on ungreased cookie sheets and flatten slightly. Bake 20 minutes or until set. Cool on cookie sheets 5 minutes. Remove to wire racks; cool completely.

6. For filling, cut remaining ½ cup butter into small pieces. Beat butter, powdered sugar, salt and 6 tablespoons milk in large bowl with electric mixer at medium speed until light and fluffy. Add additional 2 tablespoons milk, if necessary, for more spreadable filling.

7. Pipe or spread filling on flat side of vanilla cookies; top with chocolate cookies.

Chocolate Delights

CHOCOLATE STRAWBERRY STACKERS

MAKES ABOUT 20 SANDWICH COOKIES

1 cup (2 sticks) plus 6 tablespoons butter, softened, divided
2½ cups powdered sugar, divided
2 tablespoons packed brown sugar
½ teaspoon salt, divided
2 cups all-purpose flour
½ cup semisweet chocolate chips, melted
⅓ cup strawberry jam
½ teaspoon vanilla
1 to 2 tablespoons milk (optional)

1. For cookies, beat 1 cup butter, ½ cup powdered sugar, brown sugar and ¼ teaspoon salt in large bowl with electric mixer at medium speed 2 minutes or until light and fluffy. Gradually add flour, beating until blended after each addition. Beat in melted chocolate until well blended. Shape dough into 14-inch log. Wrap in plastic wrap; refrigerate 1 hour.

2. Preheat oven to 300°F. Cut log into ⅓-inch-thick slices; place on ungreased cookie sheets.

3. Bake 15 to 18 minutes or until set. Cool on cookie sheets 5 minutes. Remove to wire racks; cool completely.

4. For filling, beat remaining 6 tablespoons butter in large bowl with electric mixer at medium speed until smooth. Beat in jam, vanilla and remaining ¼ teaspoon salt until blended. Gradually add remaining 2 cups powdered sugar; beat until light and fluffy. If mixture is too thick, gradually beat in milk until desired spreading consistency is reached.

5. Pipe or spread filling on flat side of half of cookies; top with remaining cookies.

MINT CHOCOLATE DELIGHTS

MAKES 24 SANDWICH COOKIES

1½ cups all-purpose flour
¼ cup unsweetened cocoa powder
½ teaspoon salt, divided
1 cup (2 sticks) butter, softened, divided
½ cup granulated sugar
⅓ cup packed dark brown sugar
⅓ cup semisweet chocolate chips, melted and slightly cooled
1 egg
½ teaspoon vanilla
2½ cups powdered sugar
½ teaspoon mint extract
3 to 4 drops red food coloring
2 to 3 tablespoons milk or half-and-half

1. For cookies, combine flour, cocoa and ¼ teaspoon salt in small bowl. Beat ½ cup butter, granulated sugar and brown sugar in large bowl with electric mixer at medium speed until creamy. Add melted chocolate, egg and vanilla; beat until well blended. Gradually add flour mixture, beating until blended after each addition.

2. Shape dough into 16-inch log. Wrap in plastic wrap; refrigerate 1 hour or until firm.

3. Preheat oven to 400°F. Lightly grease cookie sheets. Cut log into ⅓-inch-thick slices; place 2 inches apart on prepared cookie sheets.

4. Bake 10 minutes or until set. Cool on cookie sheets 5 minutes. Remove to wire racks; cool completely.

5. For filling, beat powdered sugar, remaining ½ cup butter and ¼ teaspoon salt in large bowl with electric mixer at medium speed until well blended. Add mint extract and food coloring; beat until well blended and evenly colored. Beat in milk, 1 tablespoon at a time, until light and fluffy.

6. Pipe or spread filling on flat side of half of cookies; top with remaining cookies.

Raspberry Devil's Food Cookie Puffs

MAKES 24 SANDWICH COOKIES

1 package (about 18 ounces) devil's food cake mix
2 jars (2½ ounces each) puréed prunes
1 egg
3 tablespoons water
3 tablespoons canola oil
2 tablespoons powdered sugar
½ cup raspberry jam or fruit spread
    Powdered sugar

1. Preheat oven to 350°F. Grease cookie sheets.

2. Beat cake mix, prunes, egg, water and oil in large bowl with electric mixer at low speed until well blended. Drop dough by tablespoonfuls 2 inches apart onto prepared cookie sheets.

3. Bake 8 minutes or until cookies puff up and indent slightly when touched. Cool on cookie sheets 1 minute. Remove to wire racks; cool completely.

4. Spread 1 teaspoon jam on flat side of half of cookies; top with remaining cookies. Sprinkle with powdered sugar.

Tip

You can find small jars of puréed prunes in the baby food aisle of the supermarket.

Rocky Road Sandwiches

MAKES ABOUT 18 SANDWICH COOKIES

1 package (about 16 ounces) refrigerated chocolate chip
    cookie dough
¼ cup unsweetened cocoa powder
1 cup marshmallow creme
6 ounces cream cheese, softened
1 cup finely chopped nuts

1. For cookies, let dough stand at room temperature 15 minutes. Preheat oven to 350°F. Grease cookie sheets.

2. Beat dough and cocoa in large bowl with electric mixer at low speed until well blended. Drop dough by rounded teaspoonfuls onto prepared cookie sheets.

3. Bake 8 to 10 minutes or until set and no longer shiny. Remove to wire racks; cool completely.

4. For filling, beat marshmallow creme and cream cheese in medium bowl with electric mixer at medium speed until well blended.

5. Pipe or spread 1 tablespoon filling on flat side of half of cookies; top with remaining cookies. Press down to allow filling to squeeze out slightly.

6. Place nuts in shallow dish; roll edges of cookies in nuts to coat.

Double Chocolate Sandwich Cookies

Makes 16 Sandwich Cookies

1 package (about 16 ounces) refrigerated sugar cookie dough
1 bar (3½ to 4 ounces) bittersweet chocolate, chopped
2 teaspoons butter
¾ cup milk chocolate chips

1. For cookies, peheat oven to 350°F. Remove dough from wrapper, retaining log shape. Cut log into ¼-inch-thick slices; place 2 inches apart on ungreased cookie sheets.

2. Cut centers out of half of cookies using ½-inch round cookie cutter. (Bake centers separately or reserve for another use.)

3. Bake 10 to 12 minutes or until edges are lightly browned. Cool on cookie sheets 2 minutes. Remove to wire racks; cool completely.

4. For filling, place bittersweet chocolate and butter in small microwavable bowl. Microwave on HIGH 1½ minutes or until melted, stirring after 1 minute. Spread chocolate on flat sides of cookies without holes; immediately top with cutout cookies.

5. Place milk chocolate chips in resealable food storage bag; seal bag. Microwave on MEDIUM (50%) 1½ minutes. Turn bag; microwave 1 minute or until melted. Knead bag until chocolate is smooth.

6. Cut very small corner off bag; drizzle chocolate over sandwich cookies. Let stand about 30 minutes or until chocolate is set.

CARDAMOM-CHOCOLATE SANDWICHES

MAKES ABOUT 12 SANDWICH COOKIES

1½ cups all-purpose flour
 1 teaspoon ground cardamom
 ½ teaspoon baking soda
 ½ teaspoon salt
 ¾ cup (1½ sticks) plus 2 tablespoons butter, softened, divided
 ¾ cup packed brown sugar
 ¼ cup half-and-half
 ½ cup milk chocolate chips
 2 tablespoons milk
 1 cup sifted powdered sugar

1. For cookies, combine flour, cardamom, baking soda and salt in medium bowl. Beat ¾ cup butter and brown sugar in large bowl with electric mixer at medium speed until light and fluffy. Beat in half-and-half until blended. Gradually add flour mixture, beating until blended after each addition.

2. Spoon dough down center of sheet of waxed paper. Using sides of waxed paper, roll back and forth to form tight, smooth 10-inch log. If dough is too soft, refrigerate 1 hour and reroll log until smooth. Wrap tightly with plastic wrap; refrigerate about 4 hours or until firm. (Dough may be refrigerated up to 3 days.)

3. Preheat oven to 375°F. Cut log into ¼-inch-thick slices; place 2 inches apart on ungreased cookie sheets.

4. Bake 10 to 12 minutes or until set and edges are golden brown. Cool on cookie sheets 2 minutes. Remove to wire racks; cool completely.

5. For filling, place chocolate chips and remaining 2 tablespoons butter in medium microwavable bowl. Microwave on MEDIUM 1½ minutes or until melted, stirring after 1 minute. Stir in milk until smooth. Stir in powdered sugar until well blended.

6. Spread filling on flat side of half of cookies; top with remaining cookies.

GLUTEN-FREE CHOCOLATE SANDWICH COOKIES

MAKES 18 SANDWICH COOKIES

1 package (15 ounces) gluten-free chocolate cake mix
½ cup (1 stick) butter, melted
4 to 5 tablespoons milk, divided
1 egg
3 tablespoons unsweetened cocoa powder, divided
1 tablespoon tapioca flour
1½ cups powdered sugar
¼ cup (½ stick) butter, softened
Prepared vanilla frosting (optional)

1. For cookies, preheat oven to 350°F. Line cookie sheets with parchment paper.

2. Beat cake mix, melted butter, 2 tablespoons milk, egg, 1 tablespoon cocoa and tapioca flour in large bowl with electric mixer at medium speed 1 minute or until blended. Add additional 1 tablespoon milk, if necessary, to hold dough together.

3. Shape dough by level tablespoonfuls into balls; place 1 inch apart on prepared cookie sheets.

4. Bake 10 minutes. (Cookies will puff up and be very delicate.) Cool on cookie sheets 10 minutes. Remove to wire racks; cool completely.

5. For chocolate filling, beat powdered sugar, softened butter, remaining 2 tablespoons cocoa and 2 tablespoons milk in large bowl with electric mixer at high speed until light and fluffy.

6. Spread scant tablespoon chocolate filling on flat side of half of cookies; top with remaining cookies. If desired, use vanilla frosting instead of chocolate filling to fill half of sandwich cookies.

CHOCOLATE ALMOND MERINGUE SANDWICH COOKIES

MAKES 15 SANDWICH COOKIES

½ cup sugar, divided
¼ cup ground almonds
1 tablespoon unsweetened cocoa powder
1 teaspoon cornstarch
2 egg whites
⅛ teaspoon cream of tartar
¼ teaspoon almond extract
⅓ cup chocolate fudge topping

1. Preheat oven to 250°F. Line cookie sheets with foil; spray foil with nonstick cooking spray. Combine 3 tablespoons sugar, almonds, cocoa and cornstarch in small bowl.

2. Beat egg whites in medium bowl with electric mixer at medium speed until foamy. Add cream of tartar; beat at high speed until soft peaks form. Gradually add almond extract and remaining sugar; beat until stiff peaks form. Gently fold cocoa mixture into egg whites.

3. Drop meringue mixture by rounded teaspoonfuls about 2 inches apart onto prepared cookie sheets. (Or mixture may be piped using piping bag fitted with large tip.)

4. Bake 40 minutes. Cool on cookie sheets 2 minutes; use thin spatula to loosen cookies from foil and remove to wire racks. Cool completely.

5. Spread 1 teaspoon fudge topping on flat side of half of cookies; top with remaining cookies. Store in airtight container up to 2 days.

MINI LEMON SANDWICH COOKIES

MAKES 4½ DOZEN SANDWICH COOKIES

2 cups all-purpose flour
1¼ cups (2½ sticks) butter, softened, divided
½ cup granulated sugar, divided
⅓ cup whipping cream
1 teaspoon grated lemon peel
⅛ teaspoon lemon extract
¾ cup powdered sugar
2 to 3 teaspoons lemon juice
1 teaspoon vanilla
Yellow food coloring (optional)

1. For cookies, beat flour, 1 cup butter, ¼ cup granulated sugar, cream, lemon peel and lemon extract in large bowl with electric mixer at medium speed 2 to 3 minutes or until well blended. Divide dough into thirds. Wrap each piece in waxed paper; refrigerate until firm.

2. Preheat oven to 375°F. Place remaining ¼ cup granulated sugar in shallow bowl. Roll out each piece of dough to ⅛-inch thickness on well-floured surface. Cut out circles with 1½-inch round cookie cutter. Dip both sides of dough circles in sugar. Place 1 inch apart on ungreased cookie sheets; pierce several times with fork.

3. Bake 6 to 9 minutes or until cookies are slightly puffed but not brown. Cool on cookie sheets 1 minute. Remove to wire racks; cool completely.

4. For filling, beat powdered sugar, remaining ¼ cup butter, lemon juice and vanilla in medium bowl with electric mixer at medium speed 2 minutes or until light and fluffy. Tint with food coloring, if desired.

5. Spread ½ teaspoon filling on flat side of half of cookies; top with remaining cookies.

Burger Bliss

MAKES 24 SANDWICH COOKIES

Buns

  1 package (about 16 ounces) refrigerated sugar cookie dough
  ½ cup creamy peanut butter
  ⅓ cup all-purpose flour
  ¼ cup packed brown sugar
  ½ teaspoon vanilla
    Beaten egg white and sesame seeds (optional)

Burgers

  ½ (16-ounce) package refrigerated sugar cookie dough*
  3 tablespoons unsweetened cocoa powder
  2 tablespoons packed brown sugar
  ½ teaspoon vanilla
    Red, yellow and green decorating icings

Reserve remaining dough for another use.

1. Preheat oven to 350°F. Grease cookie sheets.

2. For buns, let 1 package dough stand at room temperature 15 minutes. Beat dough, peanut butter, flour, ¼ cup brown sugar and ½ teaspoon vanilla in large bowl with electric mixer at medium speed until well blended. Shape into 48 (1-inch) balls; place 2 inches apart on prepared cookie sheets.

3. Bake 14 minutes or until lightly browned. Brush half of cookies with egg white and sprinkle with sesame seeds after 10 minutes, if desired. Cool on cookie sheets 2 minutes. Remove to wire racks; cool completely.

4. For burgers, let ½ package dough stand at room temperature 15 minutes. Beat dough, cocoa, 2 tablespoons brown sugar and ½ teaspoon vanilla in medium bowl with electric mixer at medium speed until well blended. Shape into 24 (1-inch) balls; place 2 inches apart on prepared cookie sheets. Flatten to ¼-inch thickness.

5. Bake 12 minutes or until set. Cool on cookie sheets 2 minutes. Remove to wire racks; cool completely.

6. To assemble, use icing to attach burgers to flat sides of 24 buns. Pipe red, yellow and green icings on burgers to resemble condiments. Top with remaining buns.

LINZER SANDWICH COOKIES

MAKES ABOUT 24 SANDWICH COOKIES

1⅔ cups all-purpose flour
¼ teaspoon baking powder
¼ teaspoon salt
¾ cup granulated sugar
½ cup (1 stick) butter, softened
1 egg
1 teaspoon vanilla
   Powdered sugar
   Seedless raspberry jam

1. Combine flour, baking powder and salt in medium bowl. Beat granulated sugar and butter in large bowl with electric mixer at medium speed until light and fluffy. Beat in egg and vanilla until well blended. Gradually add flour mixture, beating at low speed until dough forms.

2. Divide dough in half. Wrap each half in plastic wrap; refrigerate 2 hours or until firm.

3. Preheat oven to 375°F. Roll out half of dough to ¼-inch thickness on lightly floured surface. Cut out circles with 1½-inch floured scalloped or plain round cookie cutters. (If dough becomes too soft, refrigerate several minutes before continuing.) Place 2 inches apart on ungreased cookie sheets.

4. Roll out remaining half of dough and cut out circles. Cut 1-inch centers of different shapes from circles; place 2 inches apart on ungreased cookie sheets.

5. Bake 7 to 9 minutes or until edges are lightly browned. Cool on cookie sheets 2 minutes. Remove to wire racks; cool completely.

6. Sprinkle powdered sugar over cookies with holes. Spread jam on flat side of whole cookies; top with sugar-dusted cookies.

PEANUTTY CREAM CHEESE PEANUT BUTTER COOKIES

MAKES 4 DOZEN SANDWICH COOKIES

3 cups all-purpose flour
2 teaspoons baking soda
½ teaspoon salt
1 cup (2 sticks) butter, softened
4 ounces cream cheese, softened
1 cup packed dark brown sugar
¾ cup granulated sugar
2 eggs
1 teaspoon vanilla
1 cup creamy peanut butter
2½ cups unsalted peanuts
Orange-Chocolate Filling (recipe follows)

1. For cookies, combine flour, baking soda and salt in medium bowl.

2. Beat butter and cream cheese in large bowl with electric mixer at medium speed until creamy. Add brown sugar and granulated sugar; beat about 4 minutes or until light and fluffy. Beat in eggs and vanilla at low speed until blended. Add peanut butter; beat until well blended. Add flour mixture; beat at low speed just until blended. Stir in peanuts. Cover and refrigerate dough 3 to 4 hours or overnight.

3. Preheat oven to 350°F. Line cookie sheets with parchment paper. Shape dough by tablespoonfuls into balls; place 1 inch apart on prepared cookie sheets.

4. Bake 8 to 10 minutes or until set. Cool on cookie sheets 2 minutes. Remove to wire racks; cool completely.

5. Prepare Orange-Chocolate Filling. Pipe or spread heaping tablespoon filling on flat side of half of cookies; top with remaining cookies.

Orange-Chocolate Filling: Beat 4 ounces softened cream cheese and ½ cup (1 stick) softened butter in large bowl with electric mixer at medium speed until smooth. Add grated peel of 1 orange and 1 tablespoon vanilla; beat at low speed until blended. Gradually add 16 ounces powdered sugar; beat at high speed 5 minutes or until light and fluffy. Beat in 4 ounces melted bittersweet chocolate until blended.

Variation: Use peanut butter or melted chocolate between the cookies for a quicker filling.

CHOCOLATE & VANILLA SANDWICH COOKIES

MAKES 22 TO 24 SANDWICH COOKIES

1¾ cups (3½ sticks) butter, softened, divided
¾ cup superfine sugar
1 egg
1½ teaspoons vanilla
2⅓ cups all-purpose flour, divided
¼ teaspoon salt
⅓ cup plus 2 tablespoons unsweetened cocoa powder, divided
4 ounces cream cheese, softened
2 cups plus 2 tablespoons powdered sugar, divided

1. For cookies, beat 1¼ cups butter and superfine sugar in large bowl with electric mixer at medium speed until creamy. Beat in egg and vanilla until well blended. Add 2 cups flour and salt; beat at low speed just until blended.

2. Remove half of dough to medium bowl; stir in remaining ⅓ cup flour. Add ⅓ cup cocoa to dough in mixer bowl; beat just until blended. Wrap doughs separately in plastic wrap; refrigerate 30 minutes or until firm.

3. Preheat oven to 350°F. Roll out plain dough to ¼-inch thickness on floured surface. Cut out 2-inch circles; place 2 inches apart on nonstick cookie sheets. Repeat with chocolate dough.

4. Bake 8 to 10 minutes. Remove to wire racks; cool completely.

5. For filling, beat remaining ½ cup butter and cream cheese in large bowl with electric mixer at medium speed until well blended. Add 2 cups powdered sugar; beat until creamy. Remove half of filling to small bowl bowl; stir in remaining 2 tablespoons powdered sugar. Add remaining 2 tablespoons cocoa to filling in mixer bowl; beat until smooth.

6. Pipe or spread chocolate filling on flat side of half of plain cookies; top with remaining plain cookies. Pipe or spread vanilla filling on flat side of half of chocolate cookies; top with remaining chocolate cookies.

Peanut Butter Aliens

MAKES 14 SANDWICH COOKIES

1 package (about 16 ounces) refrigerated sugar cookie dough
½ cup creamy peanut butter
⅓ cup all-purpose flour
¼ cup powdered sugar
½ teaspoon vanilla
   Green decorating icing
1 cup strawberry jam

1. Let dough stand at room temperature 15 minutes. Grease cookie sheets.

2. Preheat oven to 350°F. Beat dough, peanut butter, flour, powdered sugar and vanilla in large bowl with electric mixer at medium speed until well blended. Reserve half of dough; wrap and refrigerate.

3. Roll out remaining dough to ¼-inch thickness between sheets of parchment paper. Cut out 14 circles with 3-inch round cookie cutter; pinch one side of each circle to form teardrop shape. Place 2 inches apart on prepared cookie sheets.

4. Bake 12 to 14 minutes or until set. Cool on cookie sheets 2 minutes. Remove to wire racks; cool completely.

5. Roll out reserved dough to ¼-inch thickness between sheets of parchment paper. Cut out 14 circles with 3-inch round cookie cutter; pinch one side of each circle to form teardrop shape. Place 2 inches apart on prepared cookie sheets. Cut out 2 oblong holes for eyes. Make small slit for mouth.

6. Bake 12 to 14 minutes or until set. Cool on cookie sheets 2 minutes. Remove to wire racks; cool completely.

7. Spread icing on cookies with faces; let stand 10 minutes or until set. Spread jam on uncut cookies; top with iced cookies.

Orange Chai Spice Sandwich Cookies

MAKES ABOUT 24 SANDWICH COOKIES

1 package (about 18 ounces) orange cake mix
5 tablespoons butter, melted
2 eggs
1 tablespoon pumpkin pie spice
2 teaspoons ground ginger
1 teaspoon orange extract or vanilla
¼ cup cream cheese, softened
¼ cup prepared vanilla frosting
½ cup orange marmalade

1. For cookies, preheat oven to 350°F. Grease cookie sheets.

2. Beat cake mix, butter, eggs, pumpkin pie spice, ginger and orange extract in large bowl with electric mixer at low speed until well blended. Drop dough by rounded teaspoonfuls 2 inches apart onto prepared cookie sheets.

3. Bake 10 to 12 minutes or until tops are puffed and cracked. Cool on cookie sheets 5 minutes. Remove to wire racks; cool completely.

4. For filling, beat cream cheese and frosting in small bowl with electric mixer at medium speed until well blended. Stir in marmalade.

5. Pipe or spread rounded teaspoon filling on flat side of half of cookies; top with remaining cookies.

EGGS-CELLENT EASTER COOKIES
MAKES 20 SANDWICH COOKIES

1 package (about 16 ounces) refrigerated sugar cookie dough
¼ cup all-purpose flour
1 cup plus 1 tablespoon powdered sugar, divided
1 teaspoon almond extract
  Green food coloring
1 package (3 ounces) cream cheese, softened
1 tablespoon butter, softened
  Red food coloring
½ cup shredded coconut
  Colored decorating icings and gels

1. For cookies, let dough stand at room temperature 15 minutes. Preheat oven to 350°F. Grease cookie sheets.

2. Beat dough, flour, 1 tablespoon powdered sugar, almond extract and green food coloring in large bowl with electric mixer at medium speed until well blended and evenly colored.

3. Shape dough into 40 (2½-inch-long) egg shapes. Place 2 inches apart on prepared cookie sheets.

4. Bake 8 to 10 minutes or until set and edges are lightly browned. Cool on cookie sheets 2 minutes. Remove to wire racks; cool completely.

5. For filling, beat cream cheese, butter, remaining 1 cup powdered sugar and red food coloring in medium bowl with electric mixer at medium speed until smooth and evenly colored. Stir in coconut.

6. Spread filling on flat side of half of cookies; top with remaining cookies. Decorate tops of cookies with colored icings and gels as desired. Let stand until set. Refrigerate in airtight container.

HOLIDAY BUTTONS
MAKES 3½ DOZEN SANDWICH COOKIES

2 cups all-purpose flour
¼ teaspoon salt
⅛ teaspoon baking powder
1¼ cups chocolate-hazelnut spread, divided
½ cup (1 stick) butter, softened
⅓ cup granulated sugar
⅓ cup packed brown sugar
1 egg
½ teaspoon almond extract
   Decors, nonpareils or decorating sugar

1. Combine flour, salt and baking powder in medium bowl. Beat ½ cup chocolate-hazelnut spread, butter, granulated sugar and brown sugar in large bowl with electric mixer at medium speed until well blended. Add egg and almond extract; beat until well blended. Gradually add flour mixture, beating until blended after each addition.

2. Divide dough into four pieces; shape each piece into 7-inch log. Wrap in plastic wrap; refrigerate 2 to 3 hours or until firm.

3. Preheat oven to 325°F. Lightly grease cookie sheets or line with parchment paper. Cut dough into ⅜-inch-thick slices; place 1 inch apart on prepared cookie sheets. Poke 4 holes in each slice with straw.

4. Bake 12 to 14 minutes or until set. Cool on cookie sheets 1 minute. Remove to wire racks; cool completely.

5. Spread 1 teaspoon chocolate-hazelnut spread on flat side of half of cookies; top with remaining cookies. Place decors in shallow dish; roll edges of cookies in decors.

Jingle Bells Ice Cream Sandwiches

MAKES ABOUT 18 ICE CREAM SANDWICHES

1 package (about 18 ounces) devil's food cake mix
¼ cup (½ stick) plus 1 tablespoon butter, melted
3 eggs
50 hard peppermint candies, unwrapped
1 quart vanilla ice cream

1. Preheat oven to 350°F. Grease cookie sheets.

2. Beat cake mix, butter and eggs in large bowl with electric mixer at medium speed until blended and smooth. Drop dough by rounded tablespoonfuls 2 inches apart onto prepared cookie sheets.

3. Bake 12 minutes or until edges are set and tops are slightly cracked. Cool on cookie sheets 5 minutes. Remove to wire racks; cool completely.

4. Place peppermint candies in medium resealable food storage bag. Seal bag; crush candies with rolling pin or meat mallet. Place crushed candies in shallow dish.

5. Line shallow baking pan with waxed paper. Place scoop of ice cream on flat side of half of cookies; top with remaining cookies. Roll edges of sandwiches in crushed candies. Place in prepared pan; cover and freeze until ready to serve.

Tip

Ice cream is often too hard to scoop right out of the freezer. To soften it quickly, place a 1-quart container of hard-packed ice cream in the microwave and heat on MEDIUM (50%) about 20 seconds or just until softened.

CHRISTMAS WREATHS
MAKES ABOUT 18 SANDWICH COOKIES

1 package (about 16 ounces) refrigerated sugar cookie dough
2 tablespoons all-purpose flour
  Green food coloring
  Green decorating sugar or sprinkles
  Red decorating icing

1. Let dough stand at room temperature 15 minutes.

2. Beat dough, flour and food coloring in large bowl with electric mixer at medium speed until well blended and evenly colored. Divide dough in half; wrap each half in plastic wrap and freeze 20 minutes.

3. Preheat oven to 350°F. Grease cookie sheets. Roll out half of dough to ⅜-inch thickness on lightly floured surface. Cut out circles with 3-inch round or fluted cookie cutter; place 2 inches apart on prepared cookie sheets. Cut out center from each cookie with 1-inch round cookie cutter.

4. Roll out remaining half of dough to ⅜-inch thickness on lightly floured surface. Cut out circles with 3-inch round or fluted cookie cutter; place 2 inches apart on prepared cookie sheets. Cut out center from each cookie with 1-inch round cookie cutter. Cut out tiny shapes as shown in photo using hors d'oeuvre cutters, miniature cookie cutters or knife. Sprinkle with green sugar or sprinkles.

5. Bake 10 minutes or until edges are lightly browned. Cool on cookie sheets 5 minutes. Remove to wire racks; cool completely.

6. Pipe or spread icing on flat side of plain cookies; top with decorated cookies.

Metric Conversion Chart

VOLUME MEASUREMENTS (dry)

$^1/_8$ teaspoon = 0.5 mL
$^1/_4$ teaspoon = 1 mL
$^1/_2$ teaspoon = 2 mL
$^3/_4$ teaspoon = 4 mL
1 teaspoon = 5 mL
1 tablespoon = 15 mL
2 tablespoons = 30 mL
$^1/_4$ cup = 60 mL
$^1/_3$ cup = 75 mL
$^1/_2$ cup = 125 mL
$^2/_3$ cup = 150 mL
$^3/_4$ cup = 175 mL
1 cup = 250 mL
2 cups = 1 pint = 500 mL
3 cups = 750 mL
4 cups = 1 quart = 1 L

VOLUME MEASUREMENTS (fluid)

1 fluid ounce (2 tablespoons) = 30 mL
4 fluid ounces ($^1/_2$ cup) = 125 mL
8 fluid ounces (1 cup) = 250 mL
12 fluid ounces (1$^1/_2$ cups) = 375 mL
16 fluid ounces (2 cups) = 500 mL

WEIGHTS (mass)

$^1/_2$ ounce = 15 g
1 ounce = 30 g
3 ounces = 90 g
4 ounces = 120 g
8 ounces = 225 g
10 ounces = 285 g
12 ounces = 360 g
16 ounces = 1 pound = 450 g

DIMENSIONS

$^1/_{16}$ inch = 2 mm
$^1/_8$ inch = 3 mm
$^1/_4$ inch = 6 mm
$^1/_2$ inch = 1.5 cm
$^3/_4$ inch = 2 cm
1 inch = 2.5 cm

OVEN TEMPERATURES

250°F = 120°C
275°F = 140°C
300°F = 150°C
325°F = 160°C
350°F = 180°C
375°F = 190°C
400°F = 200°C
425°F = 220°C
450°F = 230°C

BAKING PAN SIZES

Utensil	Size in Inches/Quarts	Metric Volume	Size in Centimeters
Baking or Cake Pan (square or rectangular)	8×8×2	2 L	20×20×5
	9×9×2	2.5 L	23×23×5
	12×8×2	3 L	30×20×5
	13×9×2	3.5 L	33×23×5
Loaf Pan	8×4×3	1.5 L	20×10×7
	9×5×3	2 L	23×13×7
Round Layer Cake Pan	8×1½	1.2 L	20×4
	9×1½	1.5 L	23×4
Pie Plate	8×1¼	750 mL	20×3
	9×1¼	1 L	23×3
Baking Dish or Casserole	1 quart	1 L	—
	1½ quart	1.5 L	—
	2 quart	2 L	—